Status of Adivasis/Indigenous Peoples Land Series – 8

RAJASTHAN

DISCLAIMER

Status of Adivasis/Indigenous Peoples Land Series – 8

RAJASTHAN

Bhanwar Singh Chadana, Mangi Lal Gurjar,
Ginny Shrivastava and Archana Sharma

Status of Adivasis/Indigenous Peoples Land Series – 8 :
RAJASTHAN

Bhanwar Singh Chadana, Mangi Lal Gurjar,
Ginny Shrivastava and Archana Sharma

First Published, 2014

ISBN 978-93-5002-300-6

Published by
AAKAR BOOKS
28 E Pocket IV, Mayur Vihar Phase I, Delhi 110 091
Phone: 011 2279 5505 Telefax: 011 2279 5641
aakarbooks@gmail.com; www.aakarbooks.com

In association with
THE OTHER MEDIA
J 139, First Floor, Vikas Puri
New Delhi 110 018
Phones: 011 2854 3372/73, Fax: 011 4237 1129
Email: tom@theothermedia.org

Printed at
Saurabh Printers Pvt. Ltd., A 16, Sector IV, Noida

Acknowledgements

The Status of Adivasis/Indigenous Peoples (SAIP) has been an important initiative of The Other Media and All India Coordinating Forum of Adivasis/Indigenous Peoples. It began with a lot of interest and enthusiasm with a wide consultation among activists, scholars and researchers interested in Adivasis/Indigenous Peoples issues. However, the process seemed to have had its own pace and could not keep up with the expectation of completing the report on time. The present phase of the programme has covered, state-wise, issues of land and mining in the Adivasis/Indigenous Peoples areas.

This report on land issues in the Adivasi areas of Rajasthan has been prepared by Bhanwar Singh Chadana, Mangi Lal Gurjar, Ginny Shrivastava and Archana Sharma.[1] We gratefully acknowledge the efforts made by the authors and members of the Editorial Collective (EC) in preparing this report.

Members of the EC went through the report and gave their valuable comments and suggestions. We gratefully acknowledge their contribution that was available at every stage of preparation of the report. The efforts of the EC have been untiringly coordinated by C R Bijoy. The reports owe a

1. Astha, 39, Kharol Colony, Udaipur, Rajasthan, Phone : 0294-2451348, Fax : 0294-2451391 Email : astha39@gmail.com

lot to his relentless efforts to keep in the loop everyone concerned towards producing good results out of the reports. At the level of The Other Media, Ravi Hemadri, who worked as the Executive Director of the organisation through most part of the programme serves as a link between the organisation and the EC. He continued to coordinate the final editing and printing of the reports. We gratefully acknowledge the role played by both C R Bijoy and Ravi Hemadri.

We acknowledge and thank the Adivasi Academy, Tejgarh, Gujarat, and particularly Prof. Ganesh Devy, for generously hosting in February, 2008, a two-day workshop of members of the EC and authors to review the draft reports. We thank the members of the Advisory Board of the SAIP, who with their participation in the first consultation and later whenever called upon, gave their inputs to the reports. Thanks are due to Shankar Gopalakrishnan who meticulously put together statistical data and selected literature for SAIP.

Finally we would like to acknowledge and thank our funders ICCO, Netherlands, and TROCAIRE, Ireland, who supported the programme right through the last five years. We are grateful to the Foundation for Ecological Security, Anand, Gujarat, and OXFAM who generously supported the printing of reports on Land and Mining. We thank all of them for being patient with this initiative.

E Deenadayalan
General Secretary

Contents

Acknowledgements 5

List of Tables and Figures 8

Preface 9

Executive Summary 13

1. Background 15
2. Introduction 17
3. The Tribal Land Resources 22
4. The Adivasi Concept of Land Ownership 31
5. Land Alienation 47
6. Need of the Laws 62
7. Violation of Recognition of Forest Rights Act 102
8. Conclusion 117

Bibliography 119

List of Tables and Figures

Tables

1. District-wise Population of Scheduled Tribes (Census-2001) 18
2. List of STs with Population and Geographical Concentration including PTGs (2001) 20
3. Land Titles Awarded by the Court in the Feudal Period 25
4. Categories of Land in Early Mewar 26
5. Size of the Adivasi Land Holdings Compared to District Average-By District, Rajasthan 30
6. Forest Area by Legal Status (as on March 31, 2007) 94
7. Distribution of Agricultural Area Operated by SC/ST/Others (1990-91) 96
8. Some Data on Per Family Credit Taken by Families Who Took Credit 101
9. The Reasons for Taking Loans, and the Percentage of Total Loans Taken for Each Stated Purpose 101

Figures

1. Districts of Rajasthan 15
2. Dispersal of Scheduled Tribes in Rural Areas of Rajasthan State 19

Preface

Eighty-eight million Adivasis and indigenous peoples live in India—approximately one-fourth of the world's total indigenous population. Historically self-sufficient, forest-based communities with independent cultural identities they have been subjected to displacement, dispossession and repression for more than a century and are now India's poorest and most marginalised communities. Since the onset of British rule, and in many cases from much earlier, Adivasis and indigenous peoples have been systematically and forcibly dispossessed of the resources of their homelands. In gross violation of democratic practice, social justice and both constitutional and legal requirements, such dispossession continues to this day. It is also the Adivasis and indigenous peoples who have paid the heaviest price for the current neo-liberal globalisation policies, with their land, resources and forests taken from them for private capital—in the name of 'economic growth'.

These larger processes have been accompanied by the erosion and undermining of cultural identities, leading to a loss of cultural moorings and other markers of ethnicity. Less than half of India's Adivasi communities speak their own language. State and private efforts at 'mainstreaming' and against indigenous faiths, practices and cultural mores have had a devastating impact.

Such trends have not gone unchallenged. Despite

growing differentiation, ethnicity has emerged as a strong, consolidating force. Many have organised, often with the help of sympathetic outsiders, to fight against their oppressors and struggle for the control over land and other resources, and for local self-government as in parts of Central India. There have been demands for political self-determination and autonomy of varying degrees as in Jharkhand and the Northeast. The state characterises all such struggles as 'Law and Order Problems', and large parts of central India and the North-east are heavily militarised in the name of 'national security'. In other parts too state repression has been heavy and brutal.

Though these processes are well-known to many and particularly to Adivasis and indigenous people's movements, there continues to be a dearth of knowledge on the overall status of Adivasis and indigenous peoples in India. The struggle-based mass organisations of Adivasis and indigenous peoples in the Indian subcontinent articulated the need to work towards such a task in the late 1990s. The collective process to fulfil this task was launched in 2005.

The Status of Adivasis/Indigenous Peoples is conceptualised as a series of reports on salient themes affecting the lives of Adivasis/Indigenous Peoples. In the first instance, the series focuses on the situation of land and mining in the tribal tracts of the country. We hope that the series will be effective in not only deliberating upon similar themes of importance to the Adivasi present and future, but also help strengthening linkages amongst movements, activists, scholars and others who are concerned with the protection of the rights of Adivasis/Indigenous Peoples in the Indian subcontinent.

This series of reports will explore the history, the laws, and the facts, and describe struggles while providing an overview of current realities. The main purpose of these reports is to expand linkages and relationships between movements, scholars, and activists so that the future of the political struggles is informed and forward looking.

Executive Summary

This study discusses the forest and land rights, and problems of land alienation faced by the Scheduled Tribes (STs) of Rajasthan. It analyses the causes of land alienation along with an impact of the protective legislations, the land record management, and the role of the administrative machinery.

The British, in the process of bringing the Adivasi areas under their authority, also redrew the relationship between them and the non-Adivasis relegating Adivasis to a subordinate position. The loss of control over their ancestral domain initially to the British and later to the Indian state, and the non-tribals progressed. The legal provisions that were intended to deliver distributive justice, even where they were strong, in practice was largely left adrift without any political will to implement. Even the protective legislations, particularly with regard to rights to revenue and forest land, met with stiff resistance from the administration and the exploiters. Development, in the name of industrialisation or conservation, has been particularly aggressive when it comes to capture of land and natural resources. Adivasis, in particular, have had to face the brunt of this aggression.

There were revolts by the Adivasis against the British for having interfered with their traditions. Later the new set of local exploiters was targeted. With liberalisation, the assault on the land and natural resources increased. The resistance, local and national, was launched. These struggles have also seen some successes, for instance with the enactment of the Forest Rights Act at the national level and small local victories. The challenge is how to make the governments abide by the laws that they have enacted in favour of tribals.

1

Background

With an area of 342,240 sq. kms, Rajasthan became the largest state in India after Chhattisgarh was carved out of Madhya Pradesh as a new state. Rajasthan constitutes about 10.41% of the total area of the country. After the 1991 Census, five

Fig. 1: Districts of Rajasthan

more districts came into existence, namely: 1. Hanumangarh 2. Dausa 3. Rajsamand, 4. Baran and 5. Karauli. Hanumangarh was carved out from Ganganagar district, Dausa from Jaipur and Sawai Madhopur districts, Rajsamand from Udaipur district, Baran from Kota district, and Karauli from Sawai Madhopur district. The number of districts in the state went up to 32. Similarly, 28 new tehsils were created by the state government after 1991, raising the total number of tehsils to 241. However, the number of urban units remained the same at 222. The number of revenue villages also increased from 39,810 to 41,353 during the decade 1991 to 2001.

Though in terms of area, Rajasthan stood first among the states, but in terms of population the honour goes to Uttar Pradesh. According to the Census 2011, Rajasthan registered a population of 6,86,21,012 adding 1,21,47,890 to 5,64,73,122 of 2001 registering a growth rate of 21.44% during the decade. Of them, 3,56,20,086 are males and 3,30,00,926 are females.

Rajasthan is bounded on the west by Pakistan, on its north by the state of Haryana and Punjab, and the capital of India, Delhi, by Uttar Pradesh and Madhya Pradesh on its east and by Gujarat on the south.

2

Introduction

This study discusses the forest and land rights, and problems of land alienation faced by the Scheduled Tribes (STs) of Rajasthan whose interests are guaranteed in the Constitution under Article 46. It analyses the causes leading to land alienation. It discusses the legislations enacted to protect the interests of the less fortunate, the state of existing land record management, the role of the administrative machinery and the realities of land alienation which reflects the effectiveness of protective legislations.

The field study was conducted on:

1. Land eviction and land conversion in the sub-divisions of Jhadol and Udaipur.
2. Land restoration of Adivasis displaced by major dams in Salumber sub-division.
3. Land alienation and tenancy practices in the villages of Aavarda and Ganeshpura.
4. The indebtedness of Adivasis to moneylenders in the village of Bichiwada.

Data collection was quite randomly done through discussions and interviews with experienced people and Adivasi communities on the use, attachment and intimacy to their land and the history of land issues.

2.1 Adivasi Settlements

The Scheduled Area includes Dungarpur, Banswara and the Pratapgarh tehsil of Chittorgarh district. The area of tribal concentration comprises Kherwara, Kotra, Gogunda, the Phalasia tehsils of Udaipur district, the Abu Road tehsil of Sirohi district and Achnera and Arnod Panchayat samities of Chittorgarh district. The sparsely populated tribal area includes Tonk, Bhilwara and Alwar districts.

The tribal population is concentrated in the belt running from Sirohi through the Udaipur, Dungarpur, Chittorgarh and Banswara districts to the Bundi, Kota, Sawai, Madhopur, Tonk and Jaipur districts.

Table 1: District-wise Population of Scheduled Tribes (Census - 2001)

Sl. No.	*District*	*Total Population*			*Scheduled Tribes*			*ST %age to Total*
		Persons	*Male*	*Female*	*Persons*	*Male*	*Female*	
1.	Ajmer	2181670	1129920	1051750	52634	27346	25288	2.41
2.	Alwar	2992592	1586752	1405840	239905	127707	112198	8.02
3.	Banswara	1501589	760686	740903	1085272	547277	537995	72.27
4.	Baran	1021653	535137	486516	216869	113058	103811	21.23
5.	Barmer	1964835	1038247	926588	118688	62938	55750	6.04
6.	Bharatpur	2101142	1133425	967717	47077	25195	21882	2.24
7.	Bhilwara	2013789	1026650	987139	180556	93089	87467	8.97
8.	Bikaner	1674271	886075	788196	5945	3272	2673	0.36
9.	Bundi	962620	504818	457802	194851	102678	92173	20.24
10.	Chittorgarh	1803524	918063	885461	388311	197416	190895	21.53
11.	Churu	1923878	987781	936097	10063	5339	4724	0.52
12.	Dausa	1317063	693438	623625	353187	186464	166723	26.82
13.	Dholpur	983258	538103	445155	47612	25954	21658	4.84
14.	Dungarpur	1107643	547791	559852	721487	355748	365739	65.14
15.	Ganganagar	1789423	955378	834045	14744	7948	6796	0.82
16.	Hanuman-garh	1518005	801486	716519	10029	5367	4662	0.66
17.	Jaipur	5251071	2768203	2482868	412864	217546	195318	7.86
18.	Jaisalmer	508247	279101	229146	27834	14890	12944	5.48
19.	Jalore	1448940	737880	711060	126799	66610	60189	8.75
20.	Jhalawar	1180323	612804	567519	141861	74014	67847	12.02
21.	Jhunjhunu	1913689	983526	930163	36794	19054	17740	1.92
22.	Jodhpur	2886505	1513890	1372615	79540	41450	38090	2.76
23.	Kota	1568525	827128	741397	151969	80616	71353	9.69
24.	Nagaur	2775058	1424967	1350091	6497	3503	2994	0.23
25.	Pali	1820251	918856	901395	105814	54928	50886	5.81
26.	Rajsamand	987024	493459	493565	129198	65657	63541	13.09

27. Sawai Madhopur	1117057	591307	525750	241078	128446	112632	21.58
28. Karauli	1209665	651998	557667	270630	145962	124668	22.37
29. Sikar	2287788	1172753	1115035	62512	32493	30019	2.73
30. Sirohi	851107	437949	413158	210763	107905	102858	24.76
31. Tonk	1211671	626436	585235	145891	76159	69732	12.04
32. Udaipur	2633312	1336004	1297308	1260432	634953	625479	47.86
Total	56507188	29420011	27087177	7097706	3650982	3446724	12.56

Tribals of Rajasthan: Population Structure

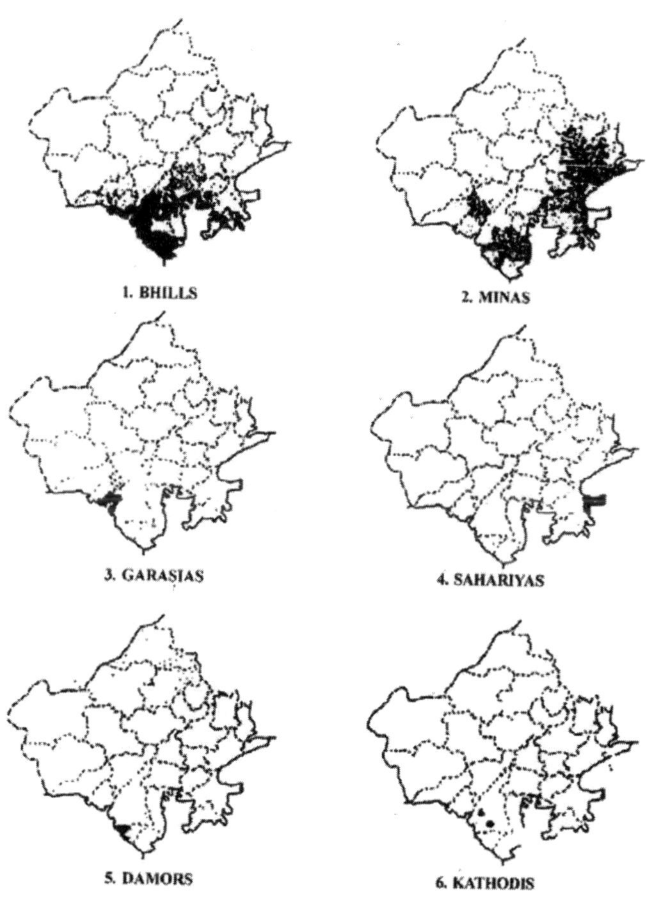

Fig. 2: Dispersal of Scheduled Tribes in Rural Areas of Rajasthan State

The Bhils are not gypsies. The Bhil country is the south-western part of Rajasthan which is mountainous and wild in the Aravallis. The Bhils live in *pals* or clusters of detached huts in the hills, each hut standing on a small mound in the midst of cultivated land. The settlement or *pal* is divided into a number of *paras* or *phalas* which afford cover and protection in case of attack. A cluster of huts within a single enclosure forms a typical Bhil habitation.

A Garasia settlement is not a cluster of houses. The dwellings are scattered over slopes of hills and mountains, and the fields extend in front of them. These solitary dwellings are made of bamboo and leaves, and lightly plastered over with cow-dung.

The Meenas who constitute almost half the tribal population used to live on rocky elevations or in thick forests, and their settlements were called *mewasas*. The cluster of their houses is also called a *pal* and is named after the *gotra* to which most of the inhabitants belonged. The Meenas were settled in the villages of Jaipur, Sawai-Madhopur and Tonk districts. Meenas consist of two communities. The Purana Basi Meenas are mostly agriculturists while the Naya Basis belongs to the light-fingered fraternity who, prior to independence, was subjected to daily attendance at the nearest police station under the Criminal Tribes Act.

Table 2: List of STs with Population and Geographical Concentration including PTGs (2001)

Sl. No.	*Tribe*	*Total Population*	*% of Tribal Population*	*Geographical Location*
1.	Meena	3, 799, 971	53.5%	Dholpur, Bharatpur, Sawai Madhopur, Karauli
2.	Bhil	2, 805, 948	39.5%	South-west Rajasthan
3.	Garasia		6.6%	
4.	Damor			
5.	Dhanka			
6.	Saharia			Shahbad, Kishangarh (Bara district)
7.	Bhil Meena		0.3%	South Rajasthan

8. Naikda		
9. Kathodi	2, 922	
10. Patelia	1, 045	
11. Kokna	405	
12. Koli Dhor	100	
Total Tribal Population	7,097,706	12.4%

Sex Ratio

As compared to the all India figures for STs, the STs of the state have a considerably lower sex ratio in total as well as in the 0-6 year group. The overall sex ratio of the ST population is 944 females per 1000 males, lower than the national average of 978 for the ST population (in 2001).

ITDP Pockets

District	*ITDP*
1. Banswara	1. Banswara
2. Dungarpur	2. Dungarpur
3. Udaipur	3. Udaipur
4. Chittorgarh	4. Chittorgarh
5. Sirohi	5. Sirohi

3

The Tribal Land Resources

3.1 Historical Context

The Adivasis of Rajasthan are amongst the 'original people' of what is now India. Not much is written about them; but before the Rajput kings started to rule, there were Adivasi chieftains who ruled the areas where they were in majority. The Meenas ruled the areas of Jaipur, Ajmer, Shahpura, Alwar, Tonk and Bundi, and the Bhils in Banswara (Bansia Bhil), Dungarpur (Dungria Bhil), Kushalgah (Kushia Bhil), Kota (Kotia Bhil).

For 600 to 1500 years, the maharajas or kings ruled their kingdoms. The King of Mewar took the support of the Adivasis to keep the Mughals out of his kingdom for over 25 years. The ancient history of the Meenas in Jaipur state is not known. However there is data on the ground situations of the Adivasi land resources in the state of Mewar in Southern Rajasthan where the Bhils lived.

The Rajput Kings ruled what is now Rajasthan. They appointed Rajput jagirdars in specified territories of the state who ruled and collected taxes on behalf of the king. The 'Jagirdari system' covered all the people in the designated area, including the Adivasi area. Since the Adivasis were relatively poor, they gave '*begar*' to the *jagirdar* (chieftains/ landowners) which are free services of all kinds. The rich farmers gave tax in cash and kind. Poor farmers gave less tax along with *begar* labour. Fifty per cent of the agricultural produce was taxed. The *jagirdar* owned the land, and the farmers, large and small, had no land ownership rights. The land owned by the *jagirdar*, and the farmers, large and small had no ownership rights. The Adivasis had their chieftains who had ruled the area, and when the Rajput warriors and the kings took over by battle and cheating, the Adivasis were chased away taking refuge in the hilly and forested areas. The good agricultural open lands and valleys were left for the ruling groups.

3.2 The Feudal System and Land Tenure

The issues of land and the feudal system are deeply entwined in the history of early Mewar. Colonial rule, which significantly influenced the power of local kings, especially their control over the peasantry, had little influence in Rajputana. As Mewar was never annexed, the feudal system continued to be the dominant definer of the state.

Land titles accrued in two fashions. While the peasantry acquired titles by clearing and tilling the land (*bhumiya* or *bapi*)[2], this was not the option open for the upper classes, especially the *jagirdars*. Land was given to them as a reward for meritorious service. Land was also given in lieu of salary to the state staff. In many cases, the award was for the revenues from land, the title remaining with the concerned peasant.[3] The quantum of land, and the nature of control over that land, defined the stature of the *jagirdar*, an important factor in an extremely status-conscious society. There were

2. Tod reports that 'he who clears, he who tills' receives the cherished title of *bhumiya* or *bapi*. Indeed, this was the only process by which titles of land could be created, and the right was respected by ruler and invader alike. The Mewar peasant said,' *Bhog na dhani raj ho, bhom na dhani ma cho'* (The court is entitled to the tax, but I have the title to my lands).
3. In such a case, the *jagirdar* would have some lands over which he would hold the *bhumiya* title, i.e. the lands of the *thikana* itself, and there would be other lands that would come into his *jagir* for revenue purposes alone.

several levels of chieftains, each with a well-defined place in court and well-defined role in governance systems. The land under the direct control of the Maharana (ruler of Mewar) was called *khalisa*, and the other lands were divided, both in terms of ownership and revenue rights, across the *jagirdars*. As stated earlier, all of them were required to collect revenue within their areas from cultivators, traders, and craftsmen, ensure law and order, etc. In addition, they were required to pay *nazrana*, perform service in lieu of *jagir* (land), provide (and seek) advice, and supply soldiers and horses. (The level of military support was of the order of two or three men and horses per Rs. 1000 of *jagir* earnings). The Rana's share in *jagir* earnings was 75%.

The Rana was the sole authority who could grant land titles, although the *jagirdars* could grant some titles for religious purposes. Land titles were awarded for the upkeep of religious buildings such as temples, mosques, etc. (*pshatdarshan*) and state apparatus (*ravli* and *patta*); for livelihood purposes to priests (*shasnik*), state staff, craftsmen and other individuals (*chakri*), and *jagirdars*. In addition, there were land gifts to *jagirdars* and others for valorous service (*bhumiya, inam*). (Tables 3 and 4)

Devasthan, *beed* grasslands, and *charnotta* are the only categories of public lands that are mentioned. Of these, the *devsthan* lands were intended for a specific purpose, and thus do not constitute a part of the commons. The *beed* lands were reserved in most cases for use by the state and its armies. *Charnots*, the village pastures, were thus the only defined village commons, with the forests in most cases being used to meet the livelihood needs of those who were being kept out of the 'land'. Some respondents report that forests too were divided into state forests and *jagir* forests, essentially being differentiated in terms of the final authority that exercised control. Of these, only the *bhumiya* and *inam* categories can be said to have had any security of tenure. The other categories were technically for the duration of state service, and continuance was at the grace of the *maharana*.

Table 3: Land Titles Awarded by the Court in the Feudal Period

Features	*Religious (Dharamarth)*		*Mafi*			*Non-religious*		
	Pshatdarshan	*Shasnik*	*Inam*	*Chakri*	*Bhum*	Grass	*Ravli*	*Patta*
Purpose	Upkeep of temple etc. Letter referred to as *Devesthan*	Livelihood of religious persons	Reward good service/ act	For duration of service	Gifts and grants normally given for valorous service. Most *Thikanas* were *bhum*	In lieu of salary while in service. Later equivalent to *bhum*.	For upkeep of Rana's family and princes	For state expenses
Revenue	Nil		Nil. The token was negotiable	Nil. Instead paid a token *nazrana*	Applicable Paid *bhumbarad* as revenue	Nil. Instead paid *Tanka* as revenue	Nil	Nil
Rights	Technically renewal but re-possession was as or a sin	Technically required renewal but re-possession was as or a sin	Could trade or mortgage	Nil. However hereditary posts meant that lands were hereditary too	Highest level of tenurial security, thus the most desired category	Nil. However hereditary posts meant that lands were hereditary too	Reverted to state on demise of person	

In addition to these tenurial forms, land was divided into several categories. The uncultivated lands (equivalent probably to today's revenue wastelands) were referred to as *bedakhila*. These could be taken over for cultivation, whereby the lands became *dakhila-kaccha*. Digging a well made the land category into *pakka.*

Table 4. Categories of Land in Early Mewar

Residential	***Padat (wastelands)***		***Agricultural Lands***		
			Kaccha	*Asli/Pakka*	
Kaccha/Pakka	*Gaucha/ Charnotta*	*Be-dakhali*	*Dakhila*	*Kham-Asami*	*Bapi*
Two categories of residential lands, for new and old villages respectively.	Reserved for grazing. Shared across many villages or panchayats. Encroachments or misuse was punished.	Equivalent to today's revenue wastelands. People encouraged bringing it under cultivation, when it became *Dakhila*.	First level of arable lands. Digging a well made it. *pakka.*	Need to cultivate for some generations to take it to the next category.	Literary hereditary. After one or two generations of use under *kham*. (Tod says, after 100 years of use)

Many lands, like the *khalisa* and *jagir* lands, were cultivated on a sharecropping basis, with shares ranging from three-fourths to one-fourth for the cultivator. Revenue on different lands was decided on the basis of the season, crop, and caste of the farmer. The 'good' agriculturists like the Jats and the Dangis paid up to two-thirds or half of the crop as revenue (*aghat*), while the 'poor' agriculturists and craftsmen were taxed at the lower levels, usually one-fourth (*chauthia*). Many communities like the Adivasis and communities who did leather work, pottery, etc. paid *bhog* and did *vet-vegar* in addition to making revenue payments. To facilitate the extraction of revenue, *patwar mandals* were established by the mid-19th century. Land settlement was undertaken between 1884 and 1886, wherein arable lands were categorised and revenues re-determined for each land.

As stated earlier, colonial rule had little or no impact on

land governance in the region. Indeed, the support provided by the British, through their cantonments in Kotra and Naseerabad, enabled the local governments to be even more ruthless regarding revenue collection. In most cases, the land deeds were in the names of the upper castes, while the actual cultivation was done by Adivasis. Furthermore, the lands cleared by Adivasis were in forest areas, where the system of land categorisation had not been applied, nor titles granted. The lands given to the Adivasis for *vet* came from the *bhum* lands of the concerned *jagirdar*. In most cases, there were no formal *pattas* issued; also, subsequent to clashes between the sovereign and the *jagirdars*, conflicting land deeds were issued, at times by those with no authority to issue them. These led to the denial of titles to actual cultivators at the time of land settlement.

There was another feature of the system that aided revenue extraction. While persons farming in *khalisa* lands were free to migrate anywhere else within the state, farmers owning lands (or farming) in *jagir* areas could move out only subsequent to the approval of the *jagirdar*. Similar rules applied to the Adivasis residing in forests falling within the *jagir* area. Thus, while in theory the *bhumiya* or *bapi* was the owner of the land, in reality even he was the servant of the *jagir*, being forced to pay ever-increasing revenues and being denied permission to leave.

In 1942, the Maharana of Mewar declared that the Adivasis living in the forest had cultivation rights to that land by decree of '*Tamra Patta*'—one '*patta*' or document per village, e.g. Pai village in Girwa Block has such a document. But after independence, the new government of Rajasthan did not consider or recognise this right to land. A number of Acts and laws were passed to bring the cultivators out from feudal systems. Among them are:

- The Rajasthan Protection of Tenancy Act, Ordinance 1949
- The Rajasthan Produce, Rent Regulating Act 1949
- The Rajasthan Land Reform and Repeal of Jagirdari

Systems Act of 1952

- The Rajasthan Forest Act 1953
- The Rajasthan Agriculture Control Act 1953
- The Rajasthan Land Summary Settlement Act 1953
- The Rajasthan Tenancy Act 1955 (that did not benefit the Adivasis much.)

The attempts to give justice and relief to the cultivators and make them 'owners', by the various laws passed between 1949 and 1952 did not yield results. The Adivasis did not get legal titles to their lands because they did not know about the laws. They also did not demand their land papers; so they remained marginalised and out of the system. The Adivasi farmers were afraid. How could they speak about their desire for their land titles to the government officials and *jagirdars* who remained in the power structure as middlemen? Thus the Adivasis remained under the influence and control of *jagirdars* and the *jagirdars* who were still the '*maliks*' or owners of their lands.

In 1953 the government of Rajasthan passed the Rajasthan Forest Act which declared that all lands that had forest on it were Forest Department land. Hillsides with a gradation of more than 30° slope would be declared forest land regardless of who cultivated it. As the Adivasis had already been pushed to the hillsides and denied valley land by the upper castes and *jagirdars;* they were the ones who lost most of their lands that they were cultivating. These lands were then designated Reserved Forest or Protected Forest. Much of the Adivasi lands that were being used by farmers for homestead and livelihood purposes went to the Forest Department. There was no record of the lands that had been used by the Adivasis. If the Adivasis had cleared the lands, cut the trees, and made flat barren lands before the Forest Act was enacted, then their farmlands would not have been declared Forest Land. In 1953, the Forest Department made their own records about what was forest land and what was agriculture land. After this Forest Act, the conflict between the Adivasis and the Forest Department began.

With the abolition of the Jagirdari System (1952), and the Rajasthan Tenancy Act (1955), whatever the Forest Department did not take, was mostly revenue land and was distributed to cultivator farmers. But the Adivasis were virtually outside this land reform and land distribution system and they are India's indigenous people living in forest areas. The exploitation and deprivation of Adivasis by the state and other powerful groups has resulted in major problems of landlessness and loss of livelihood in Adivasi communities.

According to the 2001 Census the total population of Rajasthan was 56,507,188 persons (5.5% of India's population), while its Scheduled Tribes (STs) population was 7,097,706 persons (12.6% of Rajasthan's population). Today, a high proportion of Adivasis live in forest areas of southern Rajasthan, particularly in Udaipur, Dungarpur and Banswara districts, the Kumbelgarh Block of Rajsamund district, Pratapgarh Block of Chittorgarh district, Bali and Desuri Block of Pali district and Abu Road Block of Sirohi district.

In all of Rajasthan, the decadal growth rate in population fell by 17.46% from 1971-81 to 19981-91. In Tribal Sub-Plan areas the decline was greater, falling by 26% from 1971-81 to 1981-91. This decline may be explained by the migration of the tribal population out of Sub-Plan areas to urban industrial areas in search of livelihood, largely due to the loss of control over resources traditionally used for their livelihood.[4]

While the population density per sq. km. in Rajasthan was 129, in 1991 it was only 16 for Scheduled Tribes (STs). In spite of this low density, the holdings of tribal cultivations are small, usually less than half a hectare compared with the average size of holdings of usually more than one and a half hectares in non-Adivasi districts. This is shown in the following table based on the agricultural census for the year 1995-96.

---

4. *Report of the Scheduled Areas and Scheduled Tribes Commission*, Government of India, Volume II 2002-2004, p. 722.

Table 5: Size of the Adivasi Land Holdings Compared to District Average-by District, Rajasthan

District	*No. of Adivasi Farm Families*	*No. of Hectares per Adivasi Farm*	*Average No. of Hectares per Adivasi Farm*	*District Average per Farm Family*
Jaipur and Dausa	20,342	9,923	0.49	2.75
Banswara	58,094	27,883	0.48	1.71
Chittor	19,066	10,538	0.55	1.90
Rajsamand	6,303	2,857	0.45	1.31
Sirohi	8,188	4,265	0.52	1.80
Udaipur	68,828	32,907	0.48	1.49

Non-tribals cannot sow crops on agricultural land of tribals as it would be illegal. With limited land holding, and absence of hoarding of food, the Adivasis find it difficult to meet their consumption needs.

Today most Adivasis live in rural areas and they possess some land. There are very few landless Adivasi families. They might not have the legal title to the land and their possession. The quality of the land is usually quite poor — 'hillside land, less irrigated land, rocky and stony land, and less fertile land.' But division of land amongst the children further reduced the average holding of a rural tribal family to about 2-4 *bighas*. (1 acre = 2.5 *bighas*).

4

The Adivasi Concept of Land Ownership

4.1 Land Concept

Land is at the centre of rural lives providing a household with physical, financial, and nutritional security and a labourer with wages. Land is also the basis for identity and status within a family and community. Land can also be the foundation for political power.

Both the Governments of India and Rajasthan declared various policies and laws post-independence with the main objective being rights to the people. But these did not mention the interest of Adivasis who, at the time, were described as forest dwellers or forest communities. Neither their right to the revenue land nor forest land were clarified. For these Adivasis, the forests were their habitat to which they had developed emotional attachment as their mother.

Living in harmony with their environment, both emotionally and socially, the forests was their religion, and the source of their art, music, dance, rituals, magic, myths and legends, which are intractably woven into everyday life.

Any environmental feature can be looked at in a variety of ways or environmental orientations. Broadly speaking, there are four basic environmental orientations in any culture. These are instrumental, territorial, sentimental and symbolic. By using this approach, one can clearly identify and communicate the particular factors involved in the conflict over land and forest.

The instrumental orientation considers the environment as a supply of utilisable resources. The government has so far considered the forests as a source of revenue only, while the Adivasis consider the land and forest as a primary source of food, shelter and for grazing of cattle.

The territorial orientation views space as subject to human efforts at control. The Adivasis want access to local food and material resources. They desire increasing native control of regional development. As an extension of these values, regional autonomy has become a somewhat popular theme.

The sentimental orientation focuses on the feelings of attachment to the environment. The Adivasis feel an intimate relationship with their land and the forests. This relationship shapes their sense of cultural identity. They view themselves as having always lived in a particular region and particular sites are well known for hunting, fishing, travel, burial and long-term residence. Governmental agencies have no such intimate feeling of attachment to the forests.

Through the symbolic orientations, portions of the environment have meaning that goes beyond their own manifest characteristics. In other words, they express cultural values. The Adivasis enjoy the beauty of the forests. Their music and dance are inspired by the vibrating nature of the flora and fauna that stirs their emotions. Through the moral and religious perspective, the environment is evaluated in terms of its relative sacredness. The Adivasis attribute sacred significance to the hills and the natural elements. They want their forest-based culture to be protected, but non-Adivasis do not have any such sentiments.

It is important to appreciate the difference between the conflicting environmental orientations of the Adivasis and the government. The Adivasis' orientation centres on the preservation of indigenous culture. To accomplish this goal, they must defend their habitat against the drastic alterations often associated with industrialisation, mining, irrigation and hydroelectric projects and the Forest Conservation Act. The government views forest conservation as a way to maintain environmental stability through the preservation and, where necessary, restoration of the ecological balance that has been adversely disturbed by serious deforestation which is mostly located in the Adivasi areas. This provides some of the cultural orientations underlying the conflicts in regard to the forest resources in the Adivasi region. It also provides a model, which can be used to better analyse and communicate details of such conflicts.

Land policy in post-independence India evolved through different phases. These include: two phases of land reform; attention to issues pertaining to quality of land through the Drought-Prone Area and Desert Development Programme, and Wasteland Development and Watershed Development Programme designed to reclaim environmentally degraded land. These policy interventions have had varying impacts on poverty and the overall development process. It is difficult empirically to segregate the influence of the changes in land policy on poverty, environmental management, sustainability and production; but available studies indicate that land-reform measures have had a significant impact on equity and poverty. The measures dealing with the quality of land have a partial to significant impact on environmental parameters. In addition to these, other land-policy instruments were used for the purpose of transforming development policy effectively.

For the government land is about the economic use and profit, whereas for the Adivasi, land is seen in the community interest.

4.2 Communal Land

Village community pastures (*Charagah* or *Charnot*), revenue wastelands and forests are the major common resources having potential for equitable accessibility to all classes of the rural population. Rajasthan has 1.194 million ha common pasture lands of which over 40% are extremely low in productivity or are unproductive due to excessive grazing, heavy soil erosion caused by cutting of bushes and trees, and complete neglect by the community. Apart from these pastures, there are about 0.448 million ha barren and uncultivated lands, which are also in a state of neglect. Over the decades, these lands lost their ability to facilitate regeneration of native grass and woody species. Encroachment of lands by individual families further restricted access to some of these lands.

Presently, these community pastures are not only devoid of vegetation, but also pose a threat to the livelihood of the local people by way of shortage of fodder, fuel, potable water, depletion of ground water, loss of agricultural production due to soil erosion and change in the micro-climate caused by rising temperatures and increasing wind velocity. With further reduction in precipitation and the changing pattern in rainfall distribution, the poor and small farmers in Rajasthan have gradually shifted their focus from agriculture to livestock husbandry for their livelihood, and community pastures have turned out to be the major hope for survival. However, the vested interests and powerful sections of the community, who have least concern for the poor did not have any special interest in developing those common properties. They have been changing the use of land and the government is also involved in this. The water bodies are in danger because of encroachment of land by government and land mafias, e.g. 22 *Talab* (Lake) master plan of Udaipur.

Case Study I

Encroachment of Grazing Lands

Gram Panchayat- Bedla

District- Udaipur

Village Bedla,

Total land: 1316 *bighas*, Revenue land: 513 *Bighas*, Pasture land: about 2.5 *bhigas*, Encroachment by 44 families on 200 *bighas* Revenue land.

Number of Cattle: 254, there is no communal land and this common land has been possessed illegally by influential people.

Case Study II.

Government not curbing illegal diversion of land in Kanpur Panchayat, district Udaipur.

Total land: 3362 *bighas*, Revenue land: 507 *bighas*, Pasture land: 794 *bighas*. Pasture land was allotted to RSMML (Rajasthan State Mines and Minerals) by the government. No compensation has been given to the Gram Panchayat, neither in cash nor in kind (for land). According to the norms 50 *bighas* of land are allotted as pasture land for 100 cattle. But RSMML illegally possessed 22 *bighas* Pasture land and 47 *bighas* Revenue land. This condition prevails all over Rajasthan and communal land is being converted for commercial purposes. Even 36,000 ha of forest land have been encroached for illegal mining.

4.3 The Adivasi Revolts During the 19th Century

The Adivasis' struggles during the British rule revolved around sovereignty over their land. The Bhils and Mers were the first who revolted against the new political alliance between feudalism and British imperialism in Rajasthan. By coincidence, the Mewar state signed a treaty with the British in January 1818 and the Marathas ceded the province of Ajmer to the British at the same time as they agreed to give up their rights from all the states of Rajasthan. This expanded the British Empire in Rajasthan except in the state of Sirohi which it annexed in 1823. The early policies of Ajmer compelled the Adivasis to revolt against the new order beginning from 1818. Adivasis remained in constant revolt till the end of the 19th century.

4.3.1 The Mangarh Revolt

The Govindgiri movement was named after the leader Govindgiri, a non-Adivasi born to the Banjara caste resident in the village Vedsa in Dungarpur. Socially, the movement has its origin in the great famine of 1899—*Chhapania*. During the famine, the crops failed completely and men and cattle perished in great numbers. The Christians and the Bhagats came forward to help the Bhils. Govindgiri styled himself as a monk. He declared that he was an incarnation of God and that it was his mission to reform the degenerate Bhils. He travelled in the regions of Dungarpur, Banswara, Sunt-Rampur, Idar and Panch-Mahals, which have been the Bhil land. In fact Govindgiri pressed for the processes of Sanskritisation among the Bhils. Fuchs observes:

> *He preached devotion to Rama; he forbade inter-dining with outsiders, even with Brahmins; he encouraged pious and virtuous living and the company of good people; his followers should always speak the truth, and abandon all kinds of falsehood; they should not steal, nor lust for another man's wife; they should abstain from meat and wine; they should bathe daily and wear clean clothes.*

Govindgiri was activated by a sincere desire to reform the social habits and religious beliefs of the Bhils. Through his efforts, Bhils began to emerge from their old dark and uncivilised conditions. The teachings of Govindgiri were hailed as a gospel of freedom from age-old socio-religious bandages and they came out of the state of inferiority complex. The Bhils were taught to consider themselves equals to the higher Hindu castes.

These ideas enlightened the Bhils and made them aware of their conditions and rights. These ideas also compelled them to think that they were made downtrodden by their present masters, the *Rajas* and *Thakurs*, while they were the owners of the land and ought to rule over it again. Therefore, this socio-religious reform movement culminated in the economic-politico movement.

Govindgiri became popular among the Bhils. In 1905 he established 'Samp Sabha', an organisation to unite the Bhils. The network of this *sabha* spread over a large area of Bhils. These activities alarmed the rulers, their officials and Jagirdars. They feared that Govindgiri's influence might undermine and subvert their authority. This attitude generated reactions among the Bhils. The movement gradually took a political colour. Nearly half the population of these states was under the influence of Govindgiri's movement. The immediate cause of the Bhil uprising in 1923 was the social and religious reform movement among the

Bhils under the leadership of Govindgiri. The authorities tried to suppress this social and religious reform movement with strong physical assaults. In reaction to these tyrannies of the state and jagirdars, the Bhils united to fight against them under the leadership of Govindgiri. As a result, the British suppressed the Bhils and almost 1,500 Bhils died. They had the following demands:

- Stop tax collection from Adivasis
- Liquor not to be used
- No theft
- To develop social unity and brotherhood
- Dig wells
- End *Dappa*
- *Begar* not to be given
- Be clean and bathe regularly
- Nothing like eating meat
- Also *Meribundi*
- Practise agriculture
- Men not to wear jewellery

4.3.2 Mer Revolt (1818-1821)

The Bhil and Mer revolts began coincidentally in 1881. The Mer Revolt was short-lived, while the Bhil revolt continued for a long time. The Mers were not under the direct control of any political authority, though parts of their territory were within the boundary of Mewar and Marwar states, and the Suba of Ajmer. The Mers never came under the control of the Rajputs, Mughals and Marathas. The British were the first who tried to bring them under complete subordination and this became the cause of the Mer revolt. The British wanted to impose tax which was possible only after they surrendered to the British but instead faced tough resistance before they could defeat them.

4.3.3 Meena Revolts (1851-1860)

In 1851 the Meenas of Jahajpur pargana in Udaipur state revolted against the British to show their anger and resentment towards the new order. The British brought this area under strict control of the Udaipur state. The proximity of the Meena tract to the British province of Ajmer made it possible to establish state authority. The oppression of the Mers in 1820-21 created unrest in the minds of Meenas of the Jahajpur pargana. In fact, the British were suspicious of

Adivasis and dealt with them accordingly and this led to an antagonistic feeling between the British and the Meenas. The revolts of the Meenas and Bhils were not solely against the British, but against the princely states as the British extended their policies through them.

In 1851, the Maharana of Udaipur appointed a new *hakim* (officer) of the Jahajpur pargana—Mehta Raghunath Singh— who was busy minting money from the pargana. He was mostly interested in raising the income of the pargana and reducing the expenditure. The Meenas decided to rebel against these changes. The Maharana transferred Mehta Raghunath and a new *hakim*, Mehta Ajit Singh, was appointed.

4.3.4 Bhil Revolts (1818-1860)

The Bhil tribe was known as a peaceful community, but the changes introduced by the British compelled them to revolt against the British imperialists and the native feudal order. They were enjoying undisturbed forest rights before the British rule. The majority of Bhils inhabited the former princely states of Mewar (Udaipur), Dungapur, Banswara and Sirohi of Rajasthan. In 1818, the states of Mewar (Udaipur), Dungapur and Banswara and in 1823 Sirohi concluded treaties with the British. The Bhils of Mewar state revolted against the new order that emerged out of the Mewar-British Treaty in 1818. Their numerical strength was the main source of their power to resist the well-equipped British and native forces.

Under the influence of the British rule, outsiders from plains, such as revenue officials, moneylenders, contractors, land grabbers, traders and shopkeepers, penetrated their habitation causing sufferings. They introduced new elements to poverty and imposed policies that made open the conflicts as they eroded their traditions. As they led a free life, they could not relish the semi-feudal and semi-colonial control. V.R. Raghavaiah rightly analysed that *The tribals too initiated struggle to safeguard their honour, to protect their cherished freedom and get redress against moneylenders, the zamindars, and other parasitic land holders, who tried to deprive them of all they had.* The Bhils were concerned with their racial separation and identity, economic, social and political oppression.

Practically the British became the real masters and the amount of tribute to be paid by these states was not fixed and in most of the cases, a certain portion of revenue was to be taken by the British. For instance, the amount of tribute to be paid by the Udaipur state to the British was $1/4^{th}$ up to five years, and after that it was to be raised to $3/8^{th}$ of the state's gross revenue. The rise in the state's revenue was also a rise in the company's income and the British had to try their best to raise the revenue of Mewar state. The Bhils, who were paying nominal or not paying revenue, were imposed fresh taxes. This became an important cause of Bhil revolts. Moreover, the British policy of suppression of the Bhils and other tribes compelled them to revolt.

The Bhil Revolt took place during 1861-1900. The authorities did not pacify the Bhils through redressing their grievances; rather they used force against the Bhils. The oppressive policies led the Bhils to be more turbulent. In 1861 there were reports of Bhil uprisings in Udaipur state around Kherwara and in 1863 the Bhils of Kotra (Udaipur territory) indulged in lawlessness. The Commanding Officer of Mewar Bhils Corps fixed the responsibility on Udaipur state claiming that the administrative officers were not dealing with Bhils properly.

According to the British officers the situation in the hill tracts of Udaipur was deteriorating due to negligence of the *hakim* (officer) of the district. Mehta Raghunath Singh who was appointed as the *hakim* (officer) of Magra district in 1866 was corrupt. He was later transferred to Jahajpur in 1851 as he was responsible for the Meena revolt there. The commanding officer of the Mewar Bhil Corps repeated the same charge in writing that the new *hakim* (officer) was collecting double revenue from the Bhils in an arbitrary manner through torturous means and forcibly. He was transferred and the army put an end to the Bhil disturbances.

During 1872-75, the Bhils of Banswara again rebelled for the following reasons:

- Firstly, the British and Banswara state concluded an agreement in 1868 under which the British got exclusive powers to curb the Bhils.
- Secondly, the British enhanced the amount of *Brar* tax (tribute), which the Bhils paid to the state as token of overlordship. Land revenue was imposed on the Bhils in addition to *Brar*, which they never paid previously.
- Thirdly, the state employed Makrani and *Vilaities Naukers* (Muslims and Pathans from far away north-west India, mainly from Afghanistan) to suppress the Bhils. They also lent money to the Bhils at an exorbitant rate of interest and mortgaged their children in writing. In case of non-repayment, they snatched their children and made them *Londi* (female slaves) and *Gulam* (male slaves).
- Fourthly, the severe famine during 1868-75 created unrest among the Bhils.
- And fifthly, the Bhils and Naiks of neighbouring areas of Gujarat were in revolt since 1868 which inspired the Bhils of Banswara to rebel.

Besides these accumulated grievances, there were a number of other causes for this long rebellion since 1818:

1. In 1857, the British government took over the empire from the British East India Company and a number of changes were made in Indian states, which brought checks on the rights that the Bhils enjoyed. They were not allowed to take advantage of cultivation and forest products without paying taxes, which they enjoyed freely before. The Udaipur states were reorganised.

2. To enhance land revenue, the state planned land settlement in 1878. In 1880 the settlement work began which raised doubts in the minds of the Bhils. The forest department was also established. All these caused unrest and uneasiness among the Bhils. Under the new forest rules, the forest was leased to contractors which caused suffering to the Bhils.
3. The civil officers treated the Bhils in a cruel manner and extorting money from them that some were even forced to sell their children to pay the state dues. Women, children and cattle were snatched from the Bhils if they failed to pay the state dues. In 1877 the *hakim* (officer) Pandit Raghunath Rao of Magra (Hilly tract) district was questioned by state authorities on charges of bribery and misappropriation of money.
4. The *Bania* and the moneylender who were absent in the Bhil areas were introduced under the new system. They exploited the uneducated and ignorant Bhils under the pressure of the English legal system. The revenue and civil officials, and *kalas* (liquor contractors) also engaged in moneylending in the Bhil tract. The government servants known as the *Vilayati Pathans* inflicted atrocities upon the Bhils. They used to lend Rs. 10 to the Bhils and multiply it with one hundred or two hundred and snatch their children in lieu of loans.
5. Famines of 1868-78 increased the socio-economic problems of the Bhils generating tensions. The state authorities, moneylenders, contractors and officials took full advantage of the famine.
6. The British social reforms also agitated the Bhils as witchcraft (*Dakan*) practice was prevalent among the Bhils. Any woman caught for practising witchcraft was tortured and killed. The British authority pressured the state to stop this. The Bhils saw it as an attack on their beliefs. The census operation was being conducted and this also made the Bhils suspicious as

they felt that it would lead to more taxes. They thought that they were recruiting people for the British army and the ignorant Bhils took it seriously. In March 1881, two to four thousand Bhils took an oath at Mata temple of Javad village to resist the census officials. The census of 1881 became the important cause of Bhil revolt in the Udaipur state.

7. An attack on the traditions and the autonomy of the Bhils was another important cause of Bhil revolt. Under the new arrangements, the socio-political organisations of the Bhils became defunct which was part of their life. Bhil chiefs used to settle all disputes within the Bhils, but after the formation of Magra district, the jurisdiction of civil officers was extended over these disputes. This caused inhuman and unprecedented subordination of the Bhils and disturbed their social life.
8. The revolt was also religious as they felt that the temple, Rikhabhdeo, was being taken over by the state. The hakim and the Ahalkers of the hilly district Mewar blamed and impeached the priest, Bhandari Khemraj, of the temple for misappropriation of rupees one lakh out of the temple's fund. As the Bhils were devotees of the Rikhabhdeo, they were hurt by this experience. Also it may be possible that the priest agitated the Bhils to revolt.
9. The anti-British feelings among the Bhils were also the cause of the the unrest. The British, in fact, snatched their freedom. They were under a very strict authority for the first time. The new policy in which a large number of parasitic classes and persons penetrated into the Bhil areas was also the result of the British policy. During the negotiation with the Shyamaldas in 1881, the Bhils mentioned that if the "*dardar* does not kill us, we can throw out the *firangies* from the country."

In 1881 the police atrocities ignited the spark of revolt. In the first week, an incident in the village of Padona on the Udaipur-Kherwara road gave rise to the revolt. The *Gamaties Rupa* and *Kuvera* of this village were summoned by the *Thanedar* of *Barapal* who sent a *Sewar* (constable) Akbar Husain to summon the Gamatis who refused to comply. The *Thanedar* arrived with a force which excited the Bhils. They attacked the *Thanedar*. The Police action was also related to the question of liquor distilling by the Bhils since, under the new arrangement, it was unlawful. Thus under the garb of land dispute, the *Thanedar* tried to harass the Bhils. These efforts of the *Thanedar* resulted in a formidable revolt of the Bhils.

4.3.5 Sahariyas

Saharias are the only primitive tribal people in Rajasthan. They are predominantly scattered in the Shahbad and Kishanganj tehsil in Baran district. They account for 64% of the total population.

Before 1958, the Sahariyas were bonded labourers of land owners. This land was actually in the possession of the revenue and forest departments. When the land dispute came to the fore, the dominant groups had the Sahariya land allotted in their name. It was a strangely paradoxical situation where the influential people got away with the monetary and other benefits of crops while the Sahariyas faced the brunt of the law for being 'illegal holders' of land. Whenever there was a dispute over the ownership of land, the outsider would name the Sahariya as the real owner. As a consequence of this, the Sahariya farmers and labourers associated with the land were compelled to pay fines under clause 91 of the Revenue Act.

Problems that Emerged from the Settlement of Land

The settlement campaigns undertaken during 1958-1964 threw the government records into disarray.

1. There were cases where the land of Sahariya people were registered under incorrect names.

2. The beneficiaries of the lands were never known to be peasants in the area.
3. Lands which had access to irrigation facilities were mostly appropriated by influential communities like the Sikhs and Jats.
4. The land allotted to Sahariyas had the anomaly of having overlapping *khasra* numbers, i.e. the old *khasra* number of the land existed with the new *khasra* number.
5. There were also instances where grazing and forest lands were declared as no trespasser zones.
6. There were also many cases, especially during 1961-64, where villages witnessed mass exodus of Sahariya peasants. Such abandoned villages were taken into possession by the Forest Department. When they came back to claim their lands, their demand was turned down.
7. The Revenue Department did not carry out the settlement of land that lay outside the Ceiling Act, resulting in the non-revision of documents.
8. The authorities did not undertake actual measurement of land area. The exercise was essential for denoting a new *khasra* number to the land. Thus there remained a vital gap in information as to the actual *khasra* number of the allotted land.

Although the Sahariyas are recorded to be landholders in the government documents, however the right remains restricted to the documents only. It has failed to translate into reality.

4.3.6 Meenas

According to *Encyclopedia Britannica*, 'the Meenas are possibly of inner Asiatic origin, and traditions suggest that they migrated to India in the 7th century with the Rajputs'. Scholars still disagree as to whether the Meenas are an indigenous tribe, or whether they migrated to the region from Central Asia. They form a large portion of the population in Karauli, and are numerous in Jaipur.

'Among all Meena groups, Jamindar Meenas enjoy the highest status. They claim a Kshatriya status equivalent to that of the Rajputs. In the local socio-ritual hierarchy they enjoy a clean cast status. The Jamindar Meenas are traditionally good cultivators and most of them are economically well off. They are well-integrated with other higher castes like Rajputs, Brahmins, Jats, etc.'[5]

According to the 2001 Census of Rajasthan, the total population of Meenas in Rajasthan is about 28 to 30 lakhs, i.e. 5.3% of the total population (5.65 crores). The Meenas are found concentrated particularly in Eastern districts (Jaipur, Sawai-Madhopur, Karauli, Dausa, Alwar, Tonk, etc.) and to some extent in the Hadoti region (Kota, Bundi, Jhalawad, Baran and Bhilwara).

4.3.7 Damors (Damaria)

Believed to have migrated from Gujarat with which they continue to have social contacts, the Damors are a small community of 30,603 people constituting 0.71% of the total Scheduled Tribe population of Rajasthan. They are divided into two sub-divisions, one claiming a higher descent and on that account a higher social status than the other. They reside exclusively in rural areas where they cultivate land. Their womenfolk also participate in cultivation but do not work as agricultural labourers. Because of their location on the Gujarat border and their traditional cultural affinity with Gujarat, many of them speak Gujarati. Most of them speak Wagdi, which is also a local dialect in Dungarpur.

4.3.8 Kathodias

Kathodias are a small, primitive and isolated community inhabiting Jhadol and Kotra tehsils in Udaipur district and Abu Road tehsil in Sirohi district of Rajasthan. Numerically insignificant (2, 533 according to the 1981 Census) Kathodias

5. Singh, Kumar Suresh, 1998. *People of India*. Popular Prakashan.

and other sub-groups have received special attention of the Rajasthan Government, owing to their miserable plight. The Kathodias are people of the hills and live in forests. They speak their own dialect, which is a mixture of *Wagdi* and *Marathi*. They do not originally belong to Rajasthan. Some 80 years ago, Bohras, a noted business community, impressed with Kathodias' skill at *Katha*-making persuaded about 250 families to part with their parent stock of Bhils in West Khandesh district of Bombay state in search of new fortunes in the forests of Rajasthan. They were employed in remote interior forests abounding in *Khair* trees, the raw material for manufacturing *Katha*. They thus came to be known as Kathodis or Kathodias. Presently, they are mostly engaged as labourers as they own no land or little land, and often migrate to different parts of the state and even to neighbouring Gujarat.

4.3.9 Garasias

Garasias derive their name from the Sanskrit word '*gras*' that means a morsel or subsistence. According to their tradition, over six hundred years ago the Chaughan Rajputs of Jalor, when defeated, fled to the hills where subsequently they settled on the grant subsistence. They overpowered the Bhils, the inhabitants of the region, and to pacify them also parted with some subsistence in their favour. These Bhil grant-holders came to be known as Garasias. Their settlement pattern, use of bow and arrow and the general way of life are similar to those of Bhils. They are located mostly in Sirohi, Udaipur and Pali district.

5

Land Alienation

5.1 Meaning

Tribal land alienation signifies estrangement of tribals from possession of lands. This estrangement of tribals exists both in the hills and the forests as well as the irrigated and un-irrigated plains of Rajasthan. The estrangement can be from tribals to non-tribals. Transfers of land from tribals to non-tribals are of deep concern because the impact of these transfers is at the core of land alienation.

Among various methods of land alienation is the sale, mortgage and leasing out. Protective legislation in Rajasthan encompasses all these three spheres. However, despite the protective legislation, tribal land alienation continues severely unchecked. The scattered surveys by the MLV Tribal Research and Training Institute, Udaipur, do adduce evidence to this, but no reliable and authentic study is available on this issue.

5.2 Causes of Land Alienation

5.2.1 Moneylending

Much can be said about the moneylenders in land alienation through indebtedness/mortgage for agricultural purposes. However, in the absence of ready-made packages being provided either by government schemes or commercial banks, the institution of the moneylender cannot be eliminated. Recoveries of dues by banks could have resulted in a large number of tribal land alienation despite the Supreme Court stay orders on sale of SC/ST land under the relevant Act. The restriction on the sale of SC/ST land in urban and Abadi areas is another field of interest with the conversion charges being 50% in cases of SC/CT, which has led to forged land conversion taking place.

The studies register staggering indebtedness of tribals to moneylenders. The moneylender sublets the land to the tenant himself and over a period of time becomes an absentee landlord. The rates of interest on record are 12% per annum and off record are 36% to 48% per annum.

The study in village Bichivada shows that indebtedness is universal. Of the total 421 persons who were in debt in this village, 345 belonged to STs. Among them, 73.33% had loans up to Rs. 1,000, 18.26% between Rs. 1,000 to 2,000, 6.38% between Rs. 2,000 to 3,000 and only 2.03% had taken loans of more than Rs. 3,000.

5.2.2 Loans – Major Reason of Land Alienation

In Rajasthan, the Regional Rural Banks (RRBs), Cooperatives and nationalised banks give loans under tribal welfare schemes to tribals for the purchase of agricultural machinery like water pumps, tractors, etc against the guarantee of their land. Hence they have to provide the land titles. If they fail to repay the loans, their land is auctioned off. The land auction policy of the government permits the purchase by even the non-tribals since the one who pays more secures possession of the land. In the recent case in the Thanagazi Block in Alwar District, the bank loan due to RRB was Rs. 3 lakhs. The market value of land was Rs. 50 lakhs. Since the magistrate never conducted the auction and paid the dues himself to the bank, the bank incurred a loss of Rs. 47 lakhs. The access to loans for tribals is liberal as there are no strict procedures. The rich who happen to be non-tribals take loans in the name of the tribals. Deliberately they do not repay, as they are not responsible for the loan on records. It is the tribal's responsibility; his land is auctioned and the non-tribal enjoys the benefits

5.2.3 Dams

In major dam submergence areas, the submerged lands of most major and medium irrigation projects belong to tribals. The government decided to give a permanent *Gair khatedari* status to all those whose lands are submerged in the tank beds for payment of the cash compensation. This is beneficial. Problems remain in cases where land for land has been given in distant villages. It has been seen that the entire village was shifted to non-productive areas. However, the tribals who were displaced were promised land elsewhere. Such complaints are common amongst those who belonged to sites as Kotra Block of Udaipur district in the case of Kalibor dam and Som Kagdar dam in Kherwara Block; Tidi dam in Girwa Block and many other dams in southern Rajasthan like Bisalpur, Jakham, Jawai and Mahi Dams. Further, the government machinery never follows a proper rehabilitation policy.

5.2.4 MoUs

The following MoUs were signed or are in process:

- 12,251.22 ha of land allotted for SEZ and more will be allotted without limit by the government.
- 50 lakhs ha allotted for *Ratanjote* (Jatropha).
- Apart from this, the companies have signed MoUs with the government for education, health, tourism, contract farming and the Resurgent Rajasthan Programme due to which thousands of families (mostly STs, SCs) would be displaced from their lands. These lands are being allotted to companies in the name of development.
- The government wants to make amendments in the protective laws, which will convert tribal land into non-tribal lands. There are going to be changes in the Revenue laws and the Rajasthan Bhoodaan Act.

Case Study*

- An MoU was signed by the government with the private parties and the acquisition process was started as per notice for the four villages namely, Biliya, Fanda, Dakan Kotra and Kaladvas, bordering Udaipur.
- The government took the decision to allot 15 lakh ha land for *Ratanjote* (Jatropha) and 58 thousand ha land would go to companies. This land would be allotted at Rs. 400 per ha for 30 years on lease to companies.

5.2.5 *Urbanisation*

Land conversion for commercial and residential purposes in urban and rural areas has emerged as one of the major causes of tribal land alienation. Most of these lands are situated in the urban peripheries and are tribal lands. They are being converted into residential uses and being transferred for a large sum of money to a number of other castes.

About a third of the land being converted is tribal/SC land. However, it is reported that the subsequent transactions following the conversion are in violation of Section 42-B of the Rajasthan Tenancy Act and the Registration Act and the proceedings are off the record. The recent amendment of land Act Section 90 is a great contributor to land alienation as it grants acquisition procedures to non-tribals from the tribals.

5.2.6 *Tourism*

Rajasthan is unique in many ways; very rich in historical, cultural, architectural and natural heritage. In the western half of the state, there is a vast tract of hot sandy desert, which is the most dynamic and living desert among the hot deserts of the world. Eastern half of the State is replete with historical monuments amidst very rich biodiversity of semi-arid tropical region. Above all, the people of Rajasthan are friendly and hospitable.

Rajasthan has tremendous potential of attracting foreign as well as domestic tourists. Rajasthan attracts about 25% of foreign tourists coming to India and ranks 5th in the country in this respect. The number of foreign tourists was 0.425 lakhs in 1971 which rose to 9.72 lakhs in 2004 which is likely to increase by four times at the present rate.

Impact of Tourism

1) Adverse impact on scarce water and air pollution due to factors like increase in population, number of vehicles, industrialisation, etc. The groundwater table is falling at an alarming rate in Jaipur, Udaipur, Jodhpur, Ajmer etc. Rajasthan is extremely short of water and additional demand from tourism, which is water-intensive, will be additional pressure on this scarce and precious resource.

2) Impact on civic activities

a) Pressure on Land: Providing various tourist facilities invariably causes pressure on land, e.g. use of extra land for accommodation and other infrastructure. Building materials are often extracted from the ecosystem, mostly from forests. Conversion of such extra land invariably hits three important sectors—agriculture, dairy and forests.

b) Sewage Generation and disposal planning is grossly inadequate.

c) Road Transport: The situation of traffic is already pathetic which is going to be even worse in future.

d) Socio-economic Impact: The impacts arise when tourism brings about changes in the value systems, behaviour and threatens indigenous identity. Influx of people from rural to urban areas causes social degradation, uncertainties of seasonal variations in income.

e) Environment, Wildlife and Forests: To cope with the growth in the tourism industry, large-scale constructions of roads, resorts, hotels, shops, farm houses, etc. is being taken up which causes adverse impacts like degradation of forests, soil erosion, fragmentation of wildlife habitats, encroachments, accidents, etc. Also excessive vehicular traffic, more than carrying capacity of the Protected Area, and noisy conduct of tourists cause terrible disturbance to wildlife, especially in the breeding and feeding activity. It also results in pollution, fire hazards, trampling of new regeneration, etc, within the protected area.

5.3 Background of Adivasi Land Alienation

According to Karl Marx, in a Capitalist society an alienated man lives in an alienated nature and he performs estranged labour and the product of his labour becomes alien to him. Alienation as a concept is used by many social scientists in India merely as a sociological phenomenon. Since land alienation is the crux of the depeasantisation of the Adivasis, the concept assumes utmost importance in the analysis of Adivasi rights as a part of human rights discourse. The problem of land alienation is a much deeply connected phenomenon with full of contradictions related to the existing socio-economic order. The separation of land from the Adivasi communities can be understood in a more scientific way with the assistance of the theoretical formulations of the concept of alienation.

Alienation was defined by Hegel and was used by Marx to describe and criticise a social condition in which man, far from being the active initiation of the social world, seemed more a passive object of determinate external processes. Marx says, alienation is fundamentally a particular relation of property, involving involuntary surrender to the antagonistic 'other'. Alienation is inherent in exploitative relations of production and its nature varies with that of exploitation. Hence alienation's manifestations also differ among societies based on slavery, serfdom and capitalism. Thus the concept of alienation may be interpreted to understand a specific problem of the tribals where land becomes the primordial source of exploitation and results in the creation of a society where exploitative production relations exist.

5.3.1 Forms of Land Alienation

The first and foremost is the manipulation of land records. The unsatisfactory state of land records contributes a lot to the problem of land alienation. The tribals were never legally recognised as owners of the lands which they cultivated.

The second form of land alienation is *'benami'* transfers. The report of the study team of the Union Home Ministry (May 1975) pointed out that large-scale transfers of ownership of the Adivasi lands through illegal and Benami transactions, collusive civil proceedings, etc., take place when the land remains in the names of the original owners who are reduced to the level of sharecroppers.

Another form of land alienation is related to the leasing or mortgaging of the land. To raise loans for various needs, the tribals mortgage their land to the local moneylenders or to the rich farmers.

Encroachment is another form of dispossessing the Adivasis of their lands. The new migrants are able to do this where there were no proper land records. Bribing the local *Patwari* for manipulating the date of settlement of land disputes, antedating, etc., are resorted to in order to claim the Adivasi lands.

Concubinage or marital alliance is yet another form to circumvent the law and grab Adivasi lands at no cost at all.

Fictitious adoption of the non-tribals by the tribal families is also another method to snatch the lands of the tribals.

Also the slackness in the implementation of the restrictive or protective provisions encourages the non-tribals to occupy the tribal lands. Land alienation has assumed alarming proportions. Though the problem lies elsewhere, it is unfortunately always interpreted as the handiwork of certain individuals like the moneylenders, traders, landlords, etc, without understanding the class connection of these individuals. The unsystematic land records of the pre-colonial and colonial periods continue to the present. There was collection of 'taxes', a strange phenomenon for the natives, and it was the initial process of alienation in the tribal areas.

In the name of protecting the interest of the tribals, stringent laws were enacted by the government. But the non-tribals found loopholes in them to their advantage. This double-edged nature of state policy is one of the facets of the existing contradictions in the Indian tribal society. The process of land alienation is not an accidental one; but it has arisen because of the concerted efforts of the antagonistic class interests that are operating in the Adivasi areas. This is not just migration of the non-Adivasis into Adivasi areas, rather there is a history behind this migration and the state has supported the migrant non-Adivasis to settle in the Adivasi lands.

However, being the natural owners of forests and its adjoining lands, the Adivasis are being deprived of their rights to own them. They have been relegated from their earlier 'self-reliant' status to a 'dependent' one. Coupled with the exploitation by the non-Adivasis, the state legislations also proved detrimental to their interests. Therefore to understand the root causes of the land alienation process of the Adivasi communities, its relationship with the changes in the socio-economic structures have to be understood properly.

Initially, the Adivasis were not alienated from their land; that is if we understand Indian history that the original people were the Adivasis, before even the Dravidians or Aryans. There could have been only minor skirmishes with other Adivasis. So long as land was not in scarcity, there would have been enough for all and the alienation would have been limited.

The political evolution of the Adivasis, as we could find in written literature, was that they formed into clans or tribes each with somewhat different customs. The tribes had chieftains, and it was these chieftains who came into conflict with the warrior caste in the Hindu system, of Rajputs in Rajasthan.

In all parts of the country, records relating to land are in a very bad shape. In many cases the land is recorded in the name of the person who died long ago and whose legal successors are now the owners, but their names are not entered in the records. A similar highly unsatisfactory feature exists in respect of situation of transfer of lands by acts of parties. Land goes on being transferred without consequential mutation in the records with the result that the records, as they exist and continue to exist today, hardly reflect the present day reality regarding ownership of land. Millions of cases of mutation and measurement are pending in the country.

From an economic perspective, the question of land is linked to critical issues of agricultural productivity, agrarian relations, industrial uses, infrastructure development, employment opportunities, livelihood, housing, etc. Each one of these aspects is crucial for enhancing national security by ensuring consistent economic growth, food security, export promotion, etc to reinforce the economic strength and hence, the bargaining power of the country in the international community.

5.3.2 Anupmandal Theory

Sirohi was a princely state in the southern most part of Rajasthan, bordering Gujarat, with a population consisting mainly of poor Garasia and Bhil peasants. These two communities had strong clan-based organisations, and are known for their internal solidarity and history of resistance to attempted extensions of power by princely rulers. During the 19th century, land-tax had been collected from them according to the number of ploughs owned by each family. During the first two decades of the 20th century, however, the Maharaja of Sirohi brought the area into line with British India by assessing the tax according to the area of land held by a family. The land was surveyed and title-deeds sold by auction. In most cases, Baniya usurers managed to buy these deeds, with most of the peasants becoming, in law, their 'tenants'. In this way the power of the Baniyas increased.

The cause of the Sirohi peasants was eventually taken

up by Anup Das, a local artisan who had come into contact with socialist ideas while on active service in Europe during the First World War. On his return home, he published a pamphlet in Hindi, *Jagat Hit Karini*, or 'Acting for the Good of the World', in which he described the Baniyas as *rakshasa* or 'devils', blaming them for various catastrophes such as famines, diseases, early child-deaths, and solar and lunar eclipses. In another publication, he called them *Lanka ke Dhed*, or 'untouchables from Sri Lanka'. An associate of his, Harchand Soni, composed anti-Baniya songs which were sung as *bhajan* (devotional hymns). Their aim was to stigmatise the Baniyas as aliens and foreigners to the region.

In 1920 Anup Das founded an association called the Anup Mandal, with the intention of fighting the Baniyas in a more systematic way. He also began to dress as a religious mendicant or *sadhu*. In May 1920, he held a meeting at the village of Palri attended by nearly a thousand of his followers. His most vocal supporters were members of artisan communities (notably *Suthars*, or carpenters), who often cultivated small plots of land besides carrying on their trade, but many Garasias also came. After the meeting, they marched to Sirohi town and unsuccessfully demanded an audience with the Maharaja. They then left the town and marched around the adjoining region, demanding that the Baniyas accept the teachings of Anup Das. Those who refused were assaulted and forced to hand over their supplies of grain. At the village of Padwa, they attacked a Jain *dharmsala* (rest-house), beating the Jain *sadhus* and burning some old manuscripts. After these attacks had gone on for about a week, the state authorities sent police to arrest the ringleaders. About seventy-five followers were tried, of whom forty-six were given prison sentences of between three and nine months. Those tried were a very mixed group, being drawn from the potter, carpenter, oil-presser, drummer, gardener and transporter castes, but also including Rajputs, Garasias, Dheds (untouchables) and even one Brahmin.

5.3.3 *Violation of Land Rights*

The question of land is not just the result of the existing situation. Its origin may be traced to the periods of deprivation of Adivasi lands or to periods of the withdrawal of their rights to exploit forests. Gradually, owing to various structural changes within and outside the Adivasi systems, the more advanced groups forced the Adivasis either to retreat to the nearest jungles or to become landless labourers. Though land is the only source of their livelihood, as their other assets being extremely meagre, Adivasis were severely deprived. Basically, moneylenders, traders, the feudal lords, or the rich peasants exploit the Adivasis most. It is an established fact that there is a large-scale alienation of lands, which belong to the Adivasis, and grabbers, invariably in all cases, are the non- Adivasis. This phenomenon has further intensified with the emergence of new forces of production. Commenting on this, the National Commission on Backward-Areas Development (1980) says, *'In a number of areas new industrial and mining complexes, many major irrigation projects were located in the tribal areas resulting in the submergence of extensive lands belonging to the tribals'*.

Adivasis were used extensively in the operations to denude the forest on a massive scale. This alienated the Adivasis from the forests and further widened the gap between the Adivasi landless and landed gentry of the non-Adivasi communities.

Commenting on the problem of land alienation in tribal areas, the Committee on Plan Projects, Planning Commission, presented a report on the Tribal Development Programmes in 1969. The committee noticed that tribal lands in many areas passed into the hands of non-tribals, the legal prohibitions against such transfers notwithstanding. Large-scale transfers have taken place without the permission of the collector or other competent authorities as required by law. The moneylenders exploited the loopholes and they continue to circumvent the legal provisions by entering into *'Benami'* or other clandestine transactions with the Adivasis. The impotency of legislation to arrest this growing menace to the economic advancement of the Adivasis in such a situation is thus obvious.

5.3.4 *The Modalities, Extent and Impact of Tribal Land Alienation Expropriation*

There are land struggles in progress in the outskirts of Udaipur. Four villages are being threatened with displacement to make way for Special Economic Zone (SEZ) for the stone industry (marble, granite, Kota stone, etc). These villages are Kalardwas, Beeliya, Dakin Kotra and Fanda (1,250 *bighas*). Five hundred Adivasis families are affected in these four villages. Adivasi land is being acquired near Kavita village as a training centre for the Army. The national highways running through south Rajasthan have displaced hundreds of Adivasi families from their homes, livelihood and farmlands. The issue is contemporary, not historical.

5.3.5 *Agronomics of Rajasthan: An Ideological Outlook on Land Alienation*

At the very outset it must be stated that the social structures in Rajasthan are extremely feudal and casteist, while the state's policies are socialistic. The Agrarian scenario within such a contrasting set-up needs to be examined.

The erstwhile states of Rajputana, dominated by the *Jagirdari* and *Zamindari* system, witnessed excessive peasant exploitation through rack-renting and eviction. The forest based hill-borne economies of Adivasis underwent massive changes with their migration to the plains and encapsulation by the upper caste Hindus. Despite the fact that some of the Adivasis like Bhils and Meenas were accorded the *Jagirdari* status, exploitation of peasantry continued. This period witnessed the antiquated practices of agriculture like multiple subleases and usufructuary mortgages, and a totally non-monetised wage payment and master-serf relationship oriented attitude towards agriculture existed.

The state of Rajasthan adopted the socialist approach of

Jawaharlal Nehru for abolishing rack-renting and illegal eviction from land. The idea of land ceiling and self-cultivation too were adopted. The implementation of tenancy reforms and demarcation of the tribal sub-plan areas constituted important landmarks of the socialist ideology.

5.3.6 Land Records and Role of the Administrative Machinery

The success of the basic policy of protection of tribals from land alienation is dependent on the efficacy with which land records are maintained and on the alertness of the administrative machinery at the field level. The record of rights or *Khatauni Jamabadi* and mutation register are the most important land records maintained by a *patwari* on the basis of the Rajasthan Land Records Rules, 1957. But the administrative machinery never works in the tribals' vicinity.

Alienation of Adivasi Lands to Non-Adivasis

The nature of land alienation of the Scheduled Areas is broadly of two types:

The first is the alienation of land to non-Adivasis and plainsmen, which has historically been the major form of transfer of land from Adivasis. The state was meant to play a proactive role in ensuring that tribal lands are restored back from non-tribal in this kind of exploitation. Different state governments have framed different kinds of protective laws and the results have been varied. Rajasthan has an exemplary land regulation called the land transfer Regulation Act of 1959, later amended in 1970. Despite such a strong legislation, there are a large number of pending cases where land has to be restored to the tribals. In order to effect this, what is required is:

- A strong political will to dispose of the cases.
- Transparency and access to land records at the village level to tribals in the local languages, not only in English.
- Speedy disposal of cases where tribals are involved

and oral evidence to be considered where records are absent.

- All pending land disputes should be settled immediately so that tribals do not face constant harassment from non-tribal revenue and other departments.
- Regular updating of land records, proper and regular conduct of *Jamabandhi*, display of revenue details at the village level should be implemented.
- Where lands are restored to tribals, the non-tribals get stay orders from the courts
- Tribals and non-governmental organisations (NGOs) should be allowed to participate in the process of survey of lands.
- Villages with majority tribal population adjoining Scheduled Areas should be included in Scheduled Areas; specific pockets of majority tribal (ST) population that have been excluded from Scheduled Area should be scheduled.
- Sufficient staff should be posted in the Revenue Department for speedy settlement of cases.
- All tribal villages in forest areas should be settled immediately and converted to revenue settlements.

The second important type of land alienation, an increasing trend in this decade, is state-induced tribal land alienation. The *Samata* case against the state is a classic example of how the state has been alienating tribal lands to private industries and development projects like mining, hydro-electric projects, tourism and other projects (even for schools where no tribal child is admitted). Research studies, NGOs, local Adivasi revolts and campaigns have clearly brought out the evidence that these projects have not resulted in any form of economic, social or political empowerment or progress to Adivasi communities affected by these projects. There are several serious and complex issues which need to be resolved in this connection.

Does the state have the right to alienate tribal lands to industries? This issue has been clearly settled in the *Samata* case where the Supreme Court has stated that the state is also a 'person' and therefore cannot alienate lands in the Scheduled Areas to non-tribal or private industries. Yet, even after this historic judgment directing the state to stop transfer of tribal lands to industries and to declare leases as null and void, subsequently, attempts have been made to ignore or overcome this judgment. The centre appealed to the Supreme Court for a review of the order, which was later, dismissed by the court.

6

Need of the Laws

After the medieval period of Samants exploitation, the British Rule came. The Adivasis had to face dual pressure because the British framed such rules, which were against the sovereignty and integrity of the Adivasis and also opposed their connection with nature. They narrowed the traditional rights by framing forest laws, Land Possession Act, etc. Due to this, their economic and social condition declined and got cut off from the nation's mainstream. After independence, our Constitution and policy makers tried to improve the condition of Adivasis and made provisions like the Fifth Schedule and Sixth Schedule and made laws for their rights. The laws made were clear. The former feudal class, influential and rich people, and politicians took advantage of the various protective legislations in the state amending them and finding ways to bypass them. Among these Acts were the Rajasthan Tenancy Act, Rajasthan Ceiling Act, Rajasthan Land Revenue Act, etc. Tribal areas were included under the V Schedule for the welfare of the Adivasis.

6.1 Existing Legislation and Issues in Implementation of Laws

Article 46 were the subject matter of the enactment of the Rajasthan Tenancy Act 1955 (RTA); the Registration Act 1976; the Rajasthan Relief of Agriculture Indebtedness Act 1955, the Rajasthan Moneylenders Act, 1963 and the Urban Land Conversion Rules, 1981.

6.2 Land Related Laws and Policies in the States and Their Consequences

Land Acts of Rajasthan (From 1951 to 2006)

The constitution prescribes protection and safeguards for Scheduled Tribes either specially or by way of insisting on their general rights as citizens with the object of promoting their interests. The following are the related Acts:

1. The Rajasthan Wild Animals and Protection Act, 1951
2. The Rajasthan Requisition of Land (Improvement of Agriculture Act, 1951
3. The Rajasthan Board of Revenue Ordinance (Amendment) Act 1952
4. The Rajasthan Land Reforms and Resumption of Jagirs Act, 1952
5. The Rajasthan Minor Irrigation Act 1953
6. The Rajasthan Forest Act 1953
7. The Rajasthan Lands Summary Settlement Act 1953
8. The Rajasthan Panchayati Act, 1953
9. The Rajasthan Land Acquisition Act, 1953
10. The Rajasthan Lands Special Irrigation Charges Act, 1953
11. The Rajasthan Bhoodan Yagna Act, 1954
12. The Rajasthan Religious Buildings and Places Act, 1954
13. The Rajasthan Tenancy Act, 1955
14. The Rajasthan Jagir Decisions and Proceedings (Validation) Act, 1955
15. The Rajasthan Mining Settlement Act, 1956
16. The Rajasthan Agricultural Loans Act, 1957
17. The Rajasthan Jagirdars Debt Reduction Act, 1957
18. The Rajasthan Relief of Agricultural Indebtedness Act, 1957
19. The Rajasthan Jagir Lands Resumption (Validating) Act, 1957

20. The Rajasthan Cash Jagirs Abolition Act, 1958
21. The Rajasthan Jagirdars Compensation and Rehabilitation Grants (Final Order Validation) Act, 1959
22. The Rajasthan Settlement Rents Retrospective Application (Validation) Act, 1959
23. The Rajasthan Land Revenue (Surcharge) Act, 1960
24. The Rajasthan Housing Schemes (Land Acquisition) Act, 1960
25. The Rajasthan Agricultural Produce Markets Act, 1961
26. The Rajasthan Land Reforms and Acquisition of Land-owners Estates Act, 1964
27. The Rajasthan Land and Buildings Tax Act, 1964
28. The Rajasthan Soil and Water Conservation Act, 1965
29. The Rajasthan Agricultural Produce Markets (Validating Provisions) Act, 1966
30. The Rajasthan Imposition Ceiling on Agricultural Holdings Act, 1973
31. The Rajasthan Agricultural Credit Operations (Removal of Difficulties) Act, 1974
32. The Rajasthan Land Development Corporation Act, 1975
33. The Rajasthan Lands (Restrictions on Transfer) Act, 1976
34. The Rajasthan Land Tax Act, 1985
35. The Rajasthan Panchayati Raj (Modification of Provision in Their Application to the Scheduled Areas) Act, 1999
36. The Rajasthan Farmers Participation in Management of Irrigation Systems Act, 2000
37. The RIICO Industrial Areas (Prevention of Un-Authorised Development and Encroachment) Act, 2002
38. The Rajasthan Special Economic Zones Development Act, 2003
39. The Rajasthan Land Revenue Act, 2003

Bringing certain areas under the Fifth Schedule of the Indian Constitution is of great importance to tribals. It protects and safeguards all the traditional rights of the tribals.

The Rajasthan Tenancy Act, 1955

The Rajasthan Tenancy Act 1955 (Act 3 of 1955) came into force from October 15, 1955. The Act brought uniformity in the classes of tenants and in their rights and liabilities. The Act represents one of the major steps taken by the Government of Rajasthan towards unification and reformation of divergent land tenures prevailing in different parts of the state. It was an act to consolidate and amend the law relating to tenancies of agricultural lands and to provide for certain measures of land reforms and matters connected therein. This Act can be claimed to be one of the most progressive tenancy laws of India at that time. It contains practically all the recommendations made by the Planning Commission in the First Five Year Plan. An important feature of this Act was to do away with the multiplicity of tenancies and tenures. Every person who was a tenant of land other than a sub-tenant of *Khudkasht* or as a tenant of *Khudkasht* on October 15, 1955 became a *Khatedar* tenant with heritable and transferable rights. By a subsequent amendment of Section 19 of the Act, *Khatedari* rights were also conferred by law on those tenants of the *Khudkasht* and sub-tenants whose names were recorded in the annual registers in October 1955. They were however, required to pay compensation to their landholders. Thus, with the resumption of *Jagir* lands, and abolition of *Zamindari* and *Biswedari* estates, and with the conferment of *Khatedari* rights on tenants of *Khudkasht* and sub-tenants, all tenants were brought into direct relationship with the state and heritable and transferable rights conferred on them. This was a great tribute paid to the people of Rajasthan by Mohan Lal Sukhadia, the then Chief Minister of the state.

This one provision alone is of great importance which can be hardly exaggerated. With one stroke of the pen, tenants of various categories admitted prior to October 1955 were brought on par with tenants elsewhere in the country and were conferred rights of tenancy, which were heritable and transferable. As a result, more than half a million tenants got these rights over roughly about 3 million acres of land. Besides, all payments and other cases beside rents, which were being paid by the tenants to the *jagirdars*, were also abolished.

There is some general nature of provisions in the Rajasthan Tenancy Act, which provide a shelter not only to Scheduled Castes and Scheduled Tribes but also to general castes. These are A, B, C, D, F and Sec. 34, 35, 37 S3 and 183A.

In Part One of the Tenancy Act - Baitadari (sharecropping) under Section 44 big farmers can only give some of their land for sharecropping for only five years, and at most with an extension of two years. The land to tillers was not allowed. Both these went against the tribal interest.

Land could be acquired under both the land acquisition Act 1884 and the Forest Act 1927. There was no consideration if people protested. If people go to court, they can stop the process.

The Tenancy Act was amended in 1974. *Zinswari* who writes the names of the farmers in the report stopped writing the farmers' names. Sharecroppers names are not written.

Ceiling Acts

The ceiling law was brought into force with effect from December 15, 1963. The law relating to ceiling was incorporated in the Rajasthan Tenancy Act 1955 (hereafter RTA) by introducing Chapter III-B and not by a separate law on ceiling on agricultural holdings. This legislation was not a well-thought-out one and suffered from many defects, anomalies and inequalities. The legislators continued to remove the defects from time to time, but that gave ample opportunity to landlords to evade its provisions.

Under Chapter III of the RTA, the ceiling area per family consisting of five or less members was fixed at thirty standard acres of land. Where the members of the family exceed five, the ceiling was increased for each additional member by five standard acres but not exceeding sixty standard acres of land in total.

In order to make the ceiling law more effective, the Rajasthan Imposition of Ceiling on Agricultural Holdings Act 1973 was passed becoming effective from January 1, 1973. The provisions contained in Chapter III-B of the RTA 1955 had imposed a ceiling of thirty standard acres on the holding of the agriculture land which led to the concentration of such land in the hands of a few people. The agricultural land available for cultivation in the state is limited. It was, therefore, necessary to reduce disparity and refix the ceiling limits on the agricultural holdings so that surplus agricultural land may be available for distribution to the landless. The principles for determination of ceiling law under the new law are radically different from those provided under the old law.

Section 15 of the new Act makes a provision for reopening of the cases finally decided under the old law. There was also a change in the definition of the family. Under the new Act 'family' meant a family consisting of wife, husband and their minor children. In the new ceiling laws, very few members were included in the definition of 'family'. Under the new Act, land has been classified according to the regions and different ceiling limits have been fixed for the different regions in terms of ordinary acres. The main purpose behind the enactment of the Act 1973 was to acquire the maximum area and to distribute it among the landless.

The ceiling limits defined under this Act for various categories of land for a family consisting of five or less members is as follows:

1. Land with assured irrigation and capable of growing at least two crops a year — 18 acres
2. Land with assured irrigation but capable of growing only one crop a year — 27 acres
3. Land under orchard — 54 acres

4. Land in the fertile zone but not falling in the above categories — 48 acres
5. Land in the semi-fertile zone but not falling in the above four categories — 54 acres
6. Land in the hilly zones but not falling in the above five categories — 75 acres
7. Land in the semi-desert zone but not falling in the above six categories — 125 acres
8. Land in the desert zone but not falling in the above seven categories — 175 acres

If there are more than five persons in the family, then one-sixth of the above-prescribed ceiling area will be added to the holdings of the family for every additional member, but the total land cannot exceed double of the original ceiling. Any transfer of land made by such persons shall be held ab initio void and the land will be included in the total land of the landholder for ceiling purposes.

The Rajasthan Land Revenue Allotment, Conversion and Regularisation of Agriculture Land for Residential and Commercial Purposes in Urban Areas Rules, 1981.

The Sections in the Act regarding limitations over sale of such converted land are as follows:

16. Lease of Land: On conversion or regularisation, as the case may be, the land shall be held on the basis of a lease in perpetuity. The terms and conditions of the lease shall be revisable by the government after every 99 years. The lease agreement shall be in Form C.

17. Transferability of Land: The land leased out under these rules shall be transferable subject to the conditions and restrictions provided in these rules, or by any other law or rules relating to such leases.

It seems from the Act that there are no restrictions on a tribal, who himself has converted his land for urban residential or commercial purposes, from selling it to a non-tribal. Indeed, we read in the Rajasthan Revenue Decisions 1985, the judgement in the case of Jagannath vs State of Rajasthan:

Agriculture land, converted for residential purposes according to Rules. Held transfer of such land not prohibited under the Act or Rules—No restriction on right of holders of land to transfer these so converted lands to third person. Paras 8 & 9.[6] The interpretation of this Judgement in the same document clearly states that *There is no restriction on land holders, whose land is converted from agriculture purposes to non-agriculture purposes, according to the rules, to further transfer the same converted land to third persons.*[7]

There are certain provisions, that the land to be converted should be in a certain proximity to an urban area. For Jaipur, Ajmer, Bikaner, Jodhpur and Kota, it is all agriculture lands falling within the urban agglomeration. For large cities, Udaipur, Alwar and Sri Ganganagar, it is within 3 kms of the city, and for smaller cities and towns, it is within 1 km of the municipal limits of the city/town.

It seems that it was intended to prevent tribals from being either excluded or exploited as urban areas expanded. If non-tribals were selling their land at high prices in the urban market, and tribals are restricted to sell only to other tribals, they will, in all likelihood, get much lower prices if indeed they can sell at all. Or the property dealers begin all kinds of illegal activities and fraudulent practices, and the original land owning tribal is exploited.

Rajasthan Land Revenue Conversion of Agriculture Land for Non-Agricultural Purposes in Rural Areas Rules, 1992

Agriculture land in rural areas may be converted for the following purposes:

a. Residential
b. Commercial
c. Industrial or Industrial Area
d. Salt Manufacturing
e. Public Utility

The section in the rules that deals with alienation, if the

6. The Rajasthan Revenue Decisions, 1985, p. 482.
7. Ibid., p. 482.

person converting the land is a member of a Scheduled Tribe, are as follows:

> *10. Transfer of land converted for non-agricultural purposes—Any land, duly converted for any non-agricultural purpose under these rules, and may be transferred without payment of premium or obtaining permission from the prescribed authority.*[8]

As with the Urban Conversion Rule, as long as the government gets its premium and penalty payments, it has no other 'tribal' or 'non-tribal' restriction on further and onward sale or transfer.

In many ways, these two rules, for conversion from agriculture land to non-agriculture purposes, in either urban or rural areas, nullifies the stringency of the Rajasthan Tenancy Act of 1955.

The Land Acquisition Act 1894

The Act was amended in 1984 by the central government to make certain beneficial changes in that they tried to:

- minimise the undue delays that characterise acquisition proceedings, and
- provide for payment of compensation on a realistic scale

However, it gave the government greater discretionary powers to acquire land under Section 17 (special powers in case of urgency). Land could now be acquired when it is needed for:

- a public purpose, or a company (the government has to consent to the Act being used for the Company, and the Company has to enter into specified agreements with the government (Sections 39-41)).

> A 'company' defined by the Companies Act, 1956, which includes companies in the strict sense 0f the term, societies registered under the Societies Registration Act, 1860, co-operative societies defined according to state laws and

8. Rajasthan State Current Statutes, 1992, Vol. XVII, p. 224.

industrial concerns owned by an individual or an association of Individuals.

Land can be acquired for them if needed for two purposes:

a) erecting dwelling houses or residences for workmen employed by it, or
b) providing amenities directly concerned with the above purpose, e.g. sewage, sanitation.

This is the only instance in which land can be acquired under the Act for an individual or a firm.

In the original 1894 Act (and Rajasthan, it seems, has made no state amendment), the expression of 'public purpose' includes—

(i) The provision of village-sites, or the extension, planned development or improvement of existing village-sites.
(ii) The provision of land for town or rural planning.
(iii) The provision of land for planned development of land from public funds in pursuance of any scheme or policy of government and subsequent disposal thereof in whole or in part, by lease, assignment or outright sale with the object of securing further development as planned.
(iv) The provision of land for corporation owned or controlled by the state.
(v) The provision of land for residential purposes to the poor and landless or to persons residing in areas affected by natural calamities, or to persons displaced or affected by reason of the implementation of any scheme undertaken by government, any local authority or a corporation owned or controlled by the state.
(vi) The provision of land for carrying out any educational, housing, health or slum clearance scheme sponsored by government or by any authority established by government for carrying out any such scheme, or with the prior approval of the appropriate

government, by a local authority, or a society registered under the Registration Act 1860, or under any corresponding law for the time being in force in a state, societies or a cooperative society within the meaning of any law relating to cooperative societies for the time being in force in any state.

(vii) The provision of land for any other scheme of development sponsored by government, or with the prior approval of the appropriate government, by a local authority.

(viii) The provision of any premises or building for locating a public office.

The tribal areas of Rajasthan have seen the Land Acquisition Act used to displace tribals and alienate them from their land, homes, wells, livelihoods, for dams, drinking water projects, for factories, marble cutting factories, other factories, etc. Land is acquired for mining leases granted to non-tribals to mine deposits under tribal land.

The Panchayats (Extension to the Scheduled Areas) Act, 1996 (PESA 1996)

This Act extending the provisions of Part IX of the Constitution with exceptions and modifications provided in Section 4 can be termed as 'deemed' Constitution provisions.'[9]

The Act intended to put the community back in charge of its life empowers the Gram Sabha of a village (defined as a hamlet or group of hamlets). The sections of the Act which apply most to the issue of land alienation are:

> 4. Notwithstanding anything contained under Part IX of the Constitution, the Legislature of a State shall not make any law under that Part which is inconsistent with any of the following features, namely:

9. Sharma, B.D., 1977. *Tide Turned. The Makings of Tribal Self-Rule in the First Central Law in the Wake of Bhuria Committee Report*, Sahyog Pustak Kutir, New Delhi, p. 8.

4. (d) Every Gram Sabha shall be competent to safeguard and preserve the traditions and customs of the people, their cultural identity, community resources and the customary mode of dispute resolution.

4. (i) The Gram Sabha or the Panchayats at the appropriate level shall be consulted before making the acquisition of land in the Scheduled Areas for development projects and before re-settling or rehabilitating persons affected by such projects in the Scheduled Areas; the actual planning and implementation of the projects in the Scheduled Areas shall be coordinated at the state level.

4. (k) The recommendations of the Gram Sabha or the Panchayats at the appropriate level shall be made mandatory prior to grant of prospective license or mining lease for minor minerals in the Scheduled Areas.[10]

4. (l) The prior recommendation of the Gram Sabha or the Panchayats at the appropriate level shall be made mandatory for grant of concession for the exploitation of minor minerals by auction.

4. (m) While endowing Panchayats in the Scheduled Areas with such powers and authority as may be necessary to enable them to function as institutions of self-government, a State Legislature shall ensure that the Panchayats at the appropriate level and the Gram Sabha are endowed specifically with–

ii) The ownership of minor forest produce.

iii) The power to prevent alienation of land in the Scheduled Areas and to take appropriate action to restore any unlawfully alienated land of a Scheduled Tribe.

In order to bring the State Panchayat Raj Act in compliance with PESA 1996, the Rajasthan Panchayat Raj

10. Rajasthan has most of the deposits of the minor minerals in the country. This provision will help the tribals of Rajasthan. It is noted that both Section 4. (I) and now Section 4. (k) the words 'consulted' and 'recommendation' are used. While the words are not the strongest words that could have been used, nevertheless, B.D. Sharma notes, 'that all such provisions envisaging *consultation*, in cases concerning the fundamental rights of the people, have been repeatedly interpreted by the court as a mandate for obtaining consent and not mere *performance of a ritual of reference*, Ibid., p. 18.

(Modification of Provisions in their Application to the Scheduled Areas) Act, 1999 was enacted. Though reflecting most of the provisions of PESA, almost all the powers of the Gram Sabha is 'as may be prescribed by the state government, this would mean that all the subject matters pertaining to land is subject to the rules. More than a decade later, the Rajasthan Panchayat Raj (Modification of Provisions in their Application to the Scheduled Areas) Rules was passed in 2011. In other words, PESA became operational in Rajasthan only in 2011. Therefore, it would be premature to assess its usefulness with reference to protection of land rights. However, a major glaring flaw is on the definition of the village in the state law and rules does not comply with PESA, but is constituted at the Panchayat level rather at the level of the hamlet or group of hamlets. But it must be acknowledged that Rajasthan was the second state after Himachal Pradesh to notify rules.

Scheduled Castes and Scheduled Tribes (Prevention of Atrocities) Act, 1989

As can be seen from the case study material, particularly of Southern Rajasthan, there is still a major problem of non-tribals illegally taking control of tribal land, and sometimes forcefully. Aside from appeals to the Tehsildar and SDO, the provisions of this Act can be used to reverse tribal land alienation in the state. All districts having Scheduled Areas of tribals have District Tribal Atrocity Courts, which meet regularly.

Specifically, the provisions of the Act on Atrocities on Scheduled Tribes are as follows:

> The Act is 'An Act to prevent the commission of offences of atrocities against the members of the Scheduled Castes and the Scheduled Tribes, to provide for Special Courts for the trial of such offences and for the relief and rehabilitation of the victims of such offences and for matters connected therewith or incidental thereto.'[11]

11. Singh, Gurbax, 1994.

Chapter II - Offences of Atrocities

3. Punishments for offences of atrocities— (1) Whoever, not being a member of a Scheduled Caste or a Scheduled Tribe —

(iv) Wrongfully occupies or cultivates any land owned by, or allotted to, or notified by any competent authority to be allotted to a member of a Scheduled Caste or a Scheduled Tribe or gets the land allotted to him transferred.

(v) Wrongfully dispossesses a member of a Scheduled Caste or a Scheduled Tribe from his land or interferes with the enjoyment of his rights over any land, premises or water.

(xv) Forces or causes a member of a Scheduled Caste or a Scheduled Tribe to leave his house, village or other place of residence, shall be punishable with imprisonment for a term which shall not be less than six months but which may extend to five years and with fine.

2. Whoever, not being a member of a Scheduled Caste or a Scheduled Tribe

(vii) being a public servant, commits any offence under this section, shall be punishable with imprisonment for a term which shall not be less than one year but which may extend to the punishment provided for that offence.'[12]

Supreme Court Judgement–3297, 1997 Samatha Appellant vs State of Andhra Pradesh and Others

This case challenged the right of the state to grant a mining lease (in this case, to extend the mining lease) in the Scheduled Area. The Andhra Pradesh Scheduled Area Land Transfer Regulation 1959, amended in 1970, existed to protect Scheduled Tribes from land alienation. Did the state

12. Ibid., pp. 60-61.

government have the legal right to take the land in the tribal area, and pass it on to non-tribals, in this case, Hyderabad Abrasives and Minerals (P) Ltd.? The Supreme Court decided 'No'. The principles enunciated were that the state was a 'person' wanting to take land from a tribal area, and when it was acting on behalf of a non-tribal, the character of the state was as a 'non-tribal person'.

This judgement has important ramifications for the role of the state in the Land Acquisition Act procedures, when the state acquires tribal land and passes it on to non-tribals. According to the Supreme Court judgement, such actions by the state are violations of the constitutional protection for tribal lands from alienation.

In a paper titled 'Liberalisation and Adivasis Rights' written by Girish Patel, a well-known Ahmedabad Advocate and associated with Lok Adhikar Sangh, states:

> In one of the most significant judgements (Samatha vs State of AP - AIR 1997 SC 3297), the Supreme Court, while interpreting the AP Scheduled Area Land Transfer Regulation of 1959, held that the person includes state and the state government also stands prohibited to transfer by way of lease or any other form known to law, the government land in Scheduled Areas to a non-tribal person, be it natural or juristic person except to its instrumentality or a cooperative society composed solely of tribes as is specified in the second part of S. 3(1)(a). Any other interpretation would easily defeat the purpose of exclusive power entrusted by the Fifth Schedule to the Governor.

This Supreme Court judgement is a potential legal and political tool that can be used to protect tribal land from alienation, even when the alienator is the state.

Legal Aid

When tribal land has been alienated, there is provision under the Rajasthan Tenancy Act 1955, or the Scheduled Caste and Scheduled Tribe (Prevention of Atrocities) Act 1989, to restore the land to its rightful tribal owner. Accessibility and affordability of legal assistance is an impediment; often leading the Adivasi victims to sell or mortgage their land illegally, or end up in further debt.

The Rajasthan Legal Aid Board is 'to provide free legal aid to the poor'.

The Rajasthan Revenue Department Notification Governing the Auction of Tribal Land Mortgaged to the Bank, 1998

In Rajasthan, Banks—Nationalised Banks, Scheduled Banks, Cooperative Banks, Bumi Vikas Banks—all take the land papers of the tribal borrowers at the time of finalising a loan. The land is virtually mortgaged to the Bank. Till June 1998, the rules of the Banks were that if a tribal borrower did not repay his loan, then the Bank would auction the land in its attempt to try to recover the outstanding loan amount. They could auction it and sell it to a non-tribal. The Banks and government policy too contributed to tribal land alienation.

However, with the Circular of the Revenue Department, Government of Rajasthan, Number P.5 (3) Rajasthan.-4/86 dated January 9, 1998 tribal land can only be auctioned and sold to another tribal.

Land Registry Rules Regarding Photograph, 1998

Rules have been changed requiring the photographs of both the buyer(s) and the seller(s) to be attached to the land documents when they come to the Registrar. This procedure was to apprehend those who bought land from a tribal, either legally—by getting the agriculture land converted to non-agriculture purposes, or illegally. Often, a property dealer would have taken advantage of a tribal's lack of education and awareness of the market prices, and would have purchased land from him at a cheap price. Then, in the Registrar's office, either a tribal servant (faithful and vocal), would pass for the tribal owner, or the property dealer himself would just sign 'Rama Gameti' or 'Hukma Meena'. The photographs do not completely solve the problem; it would be better to have the buyer and the seller together in person before the Registrar. But it is an attempt to remove some exploitation.

Forest Laws, Rules and Notifications Regulating Forests

As mentioned in the introductory chapter, 'tribal land' in the tribal areas also includes the Commons. The Commons are the forests, grazing land in the forests, and forest produce. The Village Forests which the kings of the princely states of Rajasthan had set aside for the use and management by the local communities, gave tribals access to forests.

However, since independence, the position of the state, be it the central government or the state government, is that the forests are government property.

The following acts surround the tribals, so that no matter which way they turn, there is a forest rule or law, which affects their lives.

- Indian Forest Act 1927 (A Central Act)
- Rajasthan Forest Act 1953 Amended 1960

Rajasthan Forest Settlement Rules 1958

This deals with the processes to delineate forest boundaries, and also to delineate the rights for people to grass, Minor Forest Produce (MFP), etc.

Rajasthan Reserved Forest Act 1960

The Reserved Forest Act restricts persons from living and farming the land in the Reserved Forest, and even to take Minor Forest Produce (MFP) is an offence liable to be punished.

Rajasthan Protected Forest Act 1980

The Protected Forest category is not quite as stringent as the Reserved Forest, but still, people need passes to take dry wood or forest produce for consumption from the forest.

Wildlife Protection Act 1972 (A Central Act)

This Act gives the Forest Department the responsibility to protect the wildlife in a game sanctuary. The Wildlife

Protection Act also says that forest dwellers or those living nearby cannot take anything from the forest for the purpose of sale. This hits poor tribal families who make a living year around by a combination of crops grown on small landholdings, daily wage labouring, and the sale of MFP. Animals have priority over people.

Rajasthan Wildlife Protection Rules 1977

These rules outline the scope and responsibilities of the Wildlife Advisory Board which is a state-level body which meets to decide about Sanctuary and National Park matters.

Rajasthan Tendu Leaf Trade Regulation Act 1974

Since all forest produce is the property of the state, and since *tendu* leaves (*beedi* leaves) are the single most lucrative forest produce for the Forest Department (it earns crores of rupees through royalty paid by contractors who bid in auctions for the right to collect leaves in the season from the state's forest), the procedures around this trade are mentioned in this Act.

Forest Conservation Act 1980 Amended 1988

This central Act provides for the conservation of forests and related and no state government or other authority can make (except with the prior approval of the central government) any order directing

(i) That any reserved forest .....shall cease to be reserved.
(ii) That any forest land or any portion thereof may be used for any non-forest purpose.
(iii) That any forest land or any portion thereof may be assigned by way of lease or otherwise to any private person or to any authority, corporation, agency or any other organisation not owned, managed or controlled by government.
(iv) That any forest land or any portion thereof may be cleared of trees which have grown naturally in that

land or portion, for the purpose of using it for reforestation.'[13]

Rajasthan Land Revenue (Allotment of Non-Agriculture Land for Private Forest Development) Act 1983 Amended 1986

Rajasthan Government, Forest Department, issued a Circular No. PO 1(18) Forest/90 dated April 24, 1991 on Solution to the Forest Land Encroachment Problem Notification Pra. Su.-3/91 dated January 24, 1991. The Notification goes on to state that:

> Statistical information compiled by the Ministry of Agriculture during the early 1980s revealed that...approximately 43 lakh ha of forest land was diverted for various purposes between 1951 and 1980, more than half of it for agriculture. The decisions of the state governments to regularise encroachments from time to time seem to have acted as strong inducement for further encroachments in forest areas.... The National Forest Policy 1988 has also observed the increasing trend in encroachments on forest land and state that these should not be regularised. The issue figured prominently at the Conference of the Forest Ministers held in May, 1989.... the following measures are suggested:
>
> 1. Pre-1980 encroachments where the state government had taken a decision before enactment of the Forest (Conservation) Act, 1980, to regularise 'eligible' category of encroachments. ....All such cases should be individually reviewed.....All encroached lands proposed for regularisation should be properly surveyed.....Encroachments proposed to be regularised must have taken place before October 25, 1980.

6.3 The Fifth Schedule and Mining

State-induced land alienation negates the very Fifth Schedule of the Constitution and also stands to question the control

13. Singh, Gayatri, Kerban Anklesaria and Colin Gonsalves (ed.) *The Environmental Activists' Handbook*, Colin Gonsalves; Bombay, p. 153.

and ownership of land and natural resources, which are essential to the tribal way of life. Alienation of land also leads to alienation of the surrounding livelihood resources, which the tribal depends on. While setting up industries and other projects, these impacts have never been taken into account or compensated. This cannot be ignored any longer.

While on the one side, tribals were alienated from their lands, on the other, there has not been any remarkable progress on health, education or infrastructure development. It has been a myth that industrialisation would lead to a corresponding improvement in these sectors among the local tribals. It has only proved that they have been further marginalised from whatever rights and resources earlier enjoyed by them. There has been no attempt to improve the skills of the tribals to compete with the mainstream societies in taking up any responsible position in the industries set up in their areas.

All projects in tribal areas were considered 'public purpose' even for private mining industries. This is the biggest fallacy of our development paradigm in tribal areas.

Further the Rajasthan Government enacted a number of laws for the tribal community, but the ground reality is that there is no proper implementation. While the Fifth Schedule is a strong frame for social security, the new economic policy as witnessed advocates its negation.

6.4 Litigation

Land alienation was studied in the villages of Aavada and Ganeshpura. There were 16 cases of sale of tribal land through normal illegal procedure to the castes and 25 cases of transfer of land from Scheduled Tribes. Besides, there were also two cases of illegal possession of mortgaged lands of tribals by non-tribals in Ganeshpura village. The tribals were reduced to the status of subtenants. The impoverished tribals lease-in hands from ex-jagirdars to subsist. The villages are often visited by droughts, which cause immense misery to the tribals. Litigation in both the tehsils of Jhadol and Udaipur and in the SDO court was seen to be very low. Only four suits of declaratory rights by tribals were incorporated. Demarcation of boundary is invariably not done. Of the allotments made from 1982-83 to 1991-1992, 23% of the allotees were other than the tribals themselves and 77 % were tribals. Equity in land allotment has been maintained. Land ceiling cases have been decided and land allotted in Jhadol village. However, to date, other allotees do not have possession.

6.5 Displacement in Scheduled Areas

Since independence, tribals displaced by development projects or industries have not been rehabilitated to date. Research shows that the number of displaced tribals till 1990 is about 85.39 lakhs (55.16% of total displaced) of whom 64.23% are yet to be rehabilitated. (Walter Fernandes, 1994). Although accurate figures of displacement vary, it is clear that the majority of those displaced have not been rehabilitated. Those displaced have been forced to migrate to new areas and most often have encroached on to forestlands and are, on record, considered illegal. It is an established fact that displacement has led to far-reaching negative social and economic consequences, not to mention the simmering disturbances and extremism in most tribal pockets. Economic planning cannot turn a blind eye to these consequences in the light of displacement.

- State-induced land alienation negates the very Fifth Schedule of the Constitution and also stands to question the control and ownership of land and natural resources, which is so essential to the tribal way of life. Alienation of land also leads to alienation of the surrounding livelihood resources, which the tribal depend on. While setting up industries and other projects these connecting impacts have never been taken into account or compensated. This cannot be ignored any longer.

- While on the one side, Adivasis were alienated from their lands, there has not been any remarkable progress on health, education or infrastructure development. It has been a myth that industrialisation would lead to a corresponding improvement in these sectors among the local Adivasis. They have been further marginalised from whatever rights and resources earlier enjoyed by them. There has been no attempt to improve the skills of the Adivasis to compete with the mainstream societies in taking up any responsible position in the industries set up in their areas.
- All projects in Adivasi areas were considered 'public purpose' even for private mining industries. This is the biggest fallacy in the development paradigm in tribal areas.

No displacement or resettlement of tribal villages for declaring any areas as national parks or sanctuaries should be allowed. The laws and policies should be adapted to strengthen coexistence and in maintaining the ecological balance.

There should not be any displacement of tribals for any project whether mining, energy or any other, in the Scheduled Areas, especially in the light of the new economic policy.

The Land Acquisition Act should be amended in consonance with the PESA Act so that rights of the people are protected in Fifth Schedule Areas.

No act of force should be used when there is conflict over resources and as per the recommendation of the 28th Report of the Scheduled Castes & Scheduled Tribes Commissioner, a law should be passed prohibiting use of force in case of disputes over resources in the tribal areas.

Government should not lease out forestlands to industries even through local institutions like Vana Samrakshana Samithis, particularly, in the Scheduled Areas (as attempted by the government of Rajasthan under GO 112).

At no cost should the Fifth and Sixth Schedule of the Constitution be amended to open up the areas for control or ownership by private non-tribal individuals, industries or institutions.

6.6 The Nature of Tribal Struggles Around Land, Including Some Recent Case Studies

6.6.1 Case Study of FLPM

Traditional rights on forest land of Adivasis in the state go back to more than 200 years. But the Mewar Royal family dominated the region for the last 1,500 years. For centuries there has been struggle for recognition of right over the forestlands; the powerful and influential people have evicted the poor people from their lands.

In southern Rajasthan the struggle has been vigorous and bloody; at times the struggle slowed down and stopped but the struggle continues.

During the British Rule, especially after the Industrial Revolution in England, the extraction from the forests to fulfil the requirement of raw material intensified. Rules framed were against the Adivasis' dignity and culture.

After independence it was expected that the tribes would get justice. But there was no amendment to the Land Allotment Act and the Forest Act. As a result, the voice of

opposition was again heard. Moreover, the Forest Conservation Act, 1980 further curtailed the Adivasis' traditional rights.

The aggression on the Adivasis increased. Evictions from their ancestral land increased. It was astonishing that the Forest Department of Rajasthan considered only 11 families as having been living prior to 1980 and the remaining thousands of Adivasi families were viewed as 'encroachers' on their own land. Atrocities against the people increased. This brutal act of injustice spurred tribals to organise against the harassments and violation of their rights by the Forest Department.

On August 19, 1995, thousands of Adivasi's living in southern Rajasthan forest areas met in Udaipur. After lengthy discussions, it was decided that in order to address the inadequacies of government commitments to rights of Adivasis, they would have to take strong united action to fight for their land rights. As a result, the Forest Land People's Movement (FLPM) was launched.

The prime responsibility of the people's movement was to give a memorandum to the tribal commissioner, to the Prime Minister demanding that the people not be evicted from their land in their possession and atrocities be stopped against them, to bring to the notice of government through rallies and sit-ins and to change the misconception that Adivasi forest dwellers have destroyed forests and that it is not just 11 but thousands of families have been dwelling in the forests before 1980. This was a serious process which could not be implemented without survey, information and mobilisation of the people into a movement. On February 6, 1996, the indefinite sit-in began in front of the Tribal Commissioner's office. The movement presented a Memorandum demanding the following:

- Identification and regularisation of Adivasi homesteads on forest lands be conducted as a well-planned implementation campaign and
- Forest Land People's Movement be recognised and

associated with the planning, implementation and monitoring of the campaign. All eviction procedures be curtailed pending regularisation and that harassment by officials be stopped.

But the Forest Department did not take any encouraging action. They continued to do nothing to identify land possessions eligible for regularisation. They were disinterested and did not want to give up their source of income. Not only this, the department did not know how many people had claims but considered only the people who had written documents of land. On this basis they again prepared a list of 5,395 families.

The FLPM was not satisfied with this list and consequently they initiated a survey on the basis of the 'Forest Conservation Act 1980 listing:

1. Cases of encroachment
2. Disputed cases
3. Cases of possession of land and lease lands
4. Forest land for conversion to Revenue Land

The Forest Land People's Movement went from village to village collecting detailed information from Adivasi families and recorded 9,000 valid possessions. The list was presented to the Tribal Commissioner challenging the data provided by the Forest Department. They continued the survey. They also stopped the no objection letter from the Forest Department to the central government that only 5,395 people had possession and the others were encroachers.

The efforts made by the campaign developed people's interest and enthusiasm in Forest Land Rights. They gained strength to stand up for their rights and struggle. Sit-ins, campaigns and rallies at village level and national level meetings were held. These gave positive results.

Those people who sat quietly, bearing the atrocities and giving bribes at every harvest, started protesting. The Government Department could not evict people because of the pressure of the movement and the people at the local level. Therefore they started giving eviction notices under

Section 91 of the 1956 Rajasthan Land Acquisition Act creating legal challenges in the court. Protests took place against this and cases were fought from the ACF court to the district level court. In Bali, ACF sentenced 16 people to jail for two months during 2006. Prior to this in the year 2002, 15 people had to spend 15 days in jail. People did not lose hope and had faith in the movement. This optimistic attitude led them to hold meetings, sit-ins, rallies, etc.

Looking at the unending legal procedures, it was felt that there are many loopholes in the Forest Conservation Act 1980 and people would not be able to get their rights as they considered only written documents and they will find ways to take advantage of Adivasis till a new law is framed in favour of Adivasis and define their traditional rights. Following this concept, the struggle in different states was brought together at the national level.

Year 2000s

On May 3, 2002 the Adivasis got the notice from the Ministry of Forests and Environment that those people who do not come under 1990 guidelines would have to be evicted from their land before September 30, 2002. Many people's organisations fighting for the rights of Adivasis protested against the Ministry of Forest and Environment. They decided to organise a campaign collectively at the national level.

Along with other organisations, the FLPM filed a writ petition in the Supreme Court as a Public Interest Litigation opposing the increase in evictions. At the same time FLPM presented a Memorandum to the Supreme Court appointed Central Empowered Committee requesting that evictions be stopped. The Ministry of Forests and Environment was compelled to issue a clarificatory order on October 30, 2002 recognising that not all forest dwellers were encroachers, and stating that occupants of land in their possessions prior to 1980 would not be evicted and that the 1990 orders should be adhered to.

In 2003 nearly 17,000 Adivasis in Udaipur, Banswara, Chittor, Dungarpur, Sirohi, Pali and Rajsamand districts, who have been in possession of forest land for generations, and whose claims had not been verified by the Forest Department, began to individually present their claims to the Collector of their respective districts. Nine thousand people submitted claims to the Collector in August 2003, so that action could be taken to establish their right over the land.

Meanwhile MoEF acknowledged in the Supreme Court in the Godavarman case that Adivasis are not encroachers on forestland, but have been living in the forests for thousands of years and should not be evicted. The historic injustices against the Adivasis should be treated with utmost urgency and a solution should evolve as soon as possible.

This proved to be a great support. In 2004, FLPM representatives of 12 states of the country convened a meeting with MoEF to discuss tribal rights over forestland and rights to forest resources. It became clear that the MoEF only passed orders and issued circulars without an effort to ensure their implementation. The state governments did not take them seriously.

A high level committee, chaired by the Prime Minister

was constituted to address the problems of tribal communities who are dependent on forests for their livelihood. This committee directed the Ministry of Tribal Affairs to draft a Tribal Forest Rights Bill that would ensure that tribal land rights are protected.

The Campaign for Survival and Dignity (CSD)[14] along with representatives of the National Advisory Council met the Prime Minister (PM). At this meeting the PM expressed his concern for the issue of rights to forest lands that are occupied and protected by Adivasi communities and the injustice against them and directed the Ministry of Tribal Affairs to draft a Tribal Forest Rights Bill that would ensure that tribal land rights are protected. A national level sit-in was held in Delhi at Jantar-Mantar in 2005. The FLPM and CSD demanded that legislation be enacted for Adivasis' rights over forestland. Forty-one Members of Parliament (MPs) from across political parties attended and gave their assurance that the Tribal Forest Rights Bill would be passed.

In September 2006, FLPM in Rajasthan with various political parties decided to take collective action in the fight for land rights. In order to address countless historic injustices done to Adivasi communities who are dependent on forests for their livelihood, the Ministry of Tribal Affairs prepared a Bill with the support of social activists and wanted to present it to the cabinet in May 2005 but was opposed and held back by the tiger and conservation lobby. The Bill was however introduced to Parliament on December 13, 2005.

The Bill presented to the Parliament was incomplete and was referred to a Joint Parliamentary Committee (JPC) of 30 members who, with the suggestions from more than 5,000 people and organisations, presented its unanimous report with significant changes to the Tribal Bill in May 2006. They expected that the Bill would be passed in the monsoon session of Parliament; but the Bill could not be passed.

---

14. A coalition of Adivasi and forest dwellers' movements at the national level that was constituted in 2002.

CSD and other organisations from across the country congregated at Jantar Mantar for a sit-in from August 21-25, 2006 demanding the passage of the Bill. This was supported by 29 MPs. On November 22, 2006, a sit-in began in front of Jantar Mantar. On November 29, a mass demonstration was held in cities—Delhi, Mumbai, Bhubaneshwar, Ranchi, and Bangalore. Over two thousand FLPM members from Rajasthan joined forest dwellers and their supporters from Madhya Pradesh and Chhattisgarh in Delhi. The rally culminated with a huge sit-in at Jantar Mantar and obtained the support of leaders of different political parties and ministers.

Pressure was created on the government and on December 15, 2006, the Forest Right Bill was presented and passed in the Lok Sabha. This Act had some loopholes due to which comparatively few people would be benefited. The Bill was passed by the Rajya Sabha and the President gave assent to it.

The people in the struggle hoped that this law would be implemented effectively. This case study is a success story of the Adivasis fighting for the land right for 12 years. Twelve years ago they did not expect this success.

6.6.2 Case Study–Bali Tehsil

In the Kurka village, Bali tehsil of Pali district, 15 tribal families worked as tenants. They earned their livelihood by cultivation of land. One day they received a notice from the Forest Department that the land they were cultivating was forestland, and they were considered as 'encroachers' on their own land. The tribal families paid no attention to this and continued the cultivation of land.

This incident took place in 2002. The tribals tried to get a stay order against the notice, but these efforts failed and the Forest Department officials destroyed the standing crops and the houses/huts of the 15 tribal families.

The forest officials took the support of people of Khetarli village and the administrative officials of Bali tehsil. And the poor tribals were evicted from their lands.

They went to the Nana Police Station to lodge the FIR. They also presented their problems to the SDM; but no action was taken.

- The standing crops and the houses/huts of tribal families were burnt and they spent the night in the open.
- The Chief Minister was also informed about it.
- They represented their problem to the National SC/ ST Commission that they had been evicted from their lands on which they had been residing for about 50 years and that they were treated inhumanly and deprived of their livelihood.
- They filed a petition at the Collector's office and orders were given for verification. When verification was done by the Forest Department reported that these were new encroachments. After this again an eviction notice was issued.
- By then orders were passed by the SC/ST Commission to provide compensation to the families whose crops and houses were burnt by the Forest Department. Nine families were given compensation. Six families were given Rs. 50,000 per family and two families were given Rs. 6,500. The total compensation amounted to Rs. 4.50 lakhs.
- The Gram Panchayat Secretary gave this amount through the Tehsildar.
- The Collector of Pali passed orders that the Forest Department cannot evict the tribals unless new laws and policies are made.

6.6.3 The Cement Factory Issue

The tribal villages of Sanmariya and Kolia in Kotra tehsil of Udaipur district lie in the midst of good forest land (reserve forest and game sanctuaries are as close as 2-12 kms). As many as 269 families live on this land that is registered in the names of 61 persons who are themselves their relatives or ancestors. Over the years, people developed their agriculture land with wells, and land levelling. A total of 292 *bighas* were used for farming and as homestead plots. This land was desired by Ranakpur Cement Factory of Kerawali Cement of Andhra Pradesh for their factory, staff quarters, offices and space for sports and welfare facilities.

The Kotra tehsil is populated by about 1,30,000 people; 86% of them are tribals who survive on small farming, daily wage labour (sometimes migrating outside the area) and collection of forest produce for sale. Cement factories are notorious for smokestack emissions of small particles of cement dust, which settle on vegetation (crop or forest) near and far, and inhibit the photosynthesis process, and retard or eliminate plant life. Any cement factory in this area would affect the income of hundreds of families in the tehsil, and of course, displace 269 families of Sanmariya and Kolia.

The Ranakpur Cement Factory contacted the Government of Rajasthan, and on behalf of the administration, the SDO of Jhadol/Kotra began land acquisition procedures with notifications to the landowners of Sanmariya and Kolia. The people got together to protest against the land acquisition, and formed the Cement Factory Struggle Committee. The people protested in writing to Section 4 and 6 of the Act, but still the process went on. The people met the Collector and the SDO, and suggested other alternative sites in the tehsil, areas of private land owned mostly by non-tribals ready to sell their land to Ranakpur Cement directly. (The law says that non-tribals cannot directly purchase tribal land, and must go through the government in a situation such as this one, but non-tribal landowners can sell directly to industry). But, the Ranakpur Cement Factory and the Government of Rajasthan chose not to consider any other site.

When the land acquisition procedures got to Section 9 on compensation claim, the people got the help of a lawyer and searched the precedents in law on this matter. The cement factory people were talking about Rs. 5,000 per *bigha* compensation for the agriculture land and no other plans for resettlement colonies, or jobs, or alternate livelihood. The search of the law books uncovered a judgement of the Patna High Court in Ashish Sahkari Nirman Samiti and others versus the State of Bihar and others, in which the principle was established that compensation for land must be calculated according to the value of the land for its future use, not the value of the land at its present use. That is to say, land that is presently agriculture land and will be used for factory land must be compensated at rates for factory or industrial land, and not at the rates for agriculture land. This makes a big difference in compensation-calculations on the basis of square footage and not on the basis of *bighas*. The SDO, Jhadol/Kotra got people's applications for land compensation claims totalling over Rs. 11 crores.

At this point, the cement factory struggle Committee filed a writ petition in the Jodhpur High Court, seeking a 'stay' in land acquisition proceedings. The stay order was granted, based on the following points:

- The Land Acquisition Act allows for the acquisition of land to extend an already existing factory or industrial site, not to build the basic factory where there is none.
- The factory site at Sanmariya and Kolia is an environmental hazard, as the site is bounded by reserve forests on all sides, and is only 12 kms from a game sanctuary.
- Consideration of the intention of the Constitution of India in the Fifth Schedule that the state should protect tribal land in tribal sub-plan areas, and act in the interest of the Scheduled Tribes.

And finally, there is the issue of the Environmental Clearance Certificate, a document required by law for any factory before construction may begin. Till now, the Ranakpur Cement Factory did not have this clearance, and the file is closed in the office of the Environment Department of the Government of Rajasthan.

This case study points out two principles: search for

alternative sites for the industry with the people (there was a complete refusal on the part of the cement factory), and stand firm with laws and policies that protect just settlements.

6.7 Forests in Rajasthan

Table 6: Forest Area by Legal Status (as on March 31, 2007)

Legal Status	*In sq. km*	*Percentage*
Reserved Forest	12453.92	38.16%
Protected Forest	17415.96	53.36%
Unclassed Forest	2768.86	8.48%
Total	32638.74	100%

The area of Rajasthan is nearly equivalent to some of the developed countries of the Western world like Norway (3,24,200 sq. kms.) Poland (3,12,600 sq. kms.) and Italy (3,01,200 sq. kms.)

The extent of natural forests in Rajasthan is not only one of the lowest in the country, but also in terms of productivity. On the contrary, the state is endowed with the largest chunk of wasteland which is about 20% of the total wastelands of the country. Keeping in view the National Forest Policy and the State Strategy on forests in order to achieve the desired forest cover, the state has twin objectives of conserving the forest areas through effective forest protection and simultaneously embark upon an ambitious afforestation programme with a conscious approach in adopting clear development strategies.

Afforestation in new areas and reforestation in areas which had lost its vegetal cover, are both a stupendous task looking to the adverse edapho-climatic conditions prevailing in most part of the state coupled with serious biotic pressure and existing socio-cultural constraints. Edapho-climatic constraints do affect the productivity and therefore, technology management is essential to enhance productivity.

But to diffuse the anthropogenic pressures on forest, judicious management strategies are to be adopted involving, local people for long-term sustainability. In order to implement such a gigantic task the human resource development and capacity building need to be undertaken in a strategic manner keeping in view the paradigm change. Forestry research needs to be strengthened towards desired goals of higher productivity, technology improvement and cost effectiveness in forestry practices.

Forestry in the state cannot be implemented through a departmental programme alone unless it is taken up as the people's movement for which the Forest Department can only act as a facilitator through their continued efforts in communication, extension and publicity. Moreover realising the stupendous task before the government, financial inputs should be stepped up in a phased manner at least in proportions to the sectoral contribution in the state's domestic product.

6.7 Agriculture in Rajasthan

Table 7: Distribution of Agricultural Area Operated by SC/ST/ Others (1990-91)

	Scheduled Caste		*Scheduled Tribes*		*Others*		*All Social Groups*	
	Area	*%*	*Area*	*%*	*Area*	*%*	*Area*	*%*
Rajasthan	2464	11.75	1759	8.39	16748	79.86	20971	100
India	13173	7.96	17908	10.82	134426	81.22	165507	100

Source: Lok Sabha Unstarred Q. No. 6962, Dated May 11, 2000.

Rajasthan's economy is mainly agriculture-based. About 80% of the population lives in rural areas and is dependent on farming. The agricultural sector of the state accounts for 22.5%. The arid state which receives not more than an annual rainfall of 25 cms thrives on agriculture that is carried out with irrigation systems and painstaking efforts of the poor farmers of Rajasthan. As a major portion of the state is parched and infertile, agriculture becomes very difficult.

Though there are vast tracts of the desert in western Rajasthan, the ecological environment is semi-arid; in eastern Rajasthan, where rivers and a lush green cover are present, there is more rain, and the seasonal crops are plentiful. In these harsh climatic conditions, women tend to the cattle and their milking, while the elderly or the young take them out to pastures for grazing. In the past, when agriculture was a risky affair, it became necessary to raise cattle for survival, a tradition that has continued to grow, turning Rajasthan into one of the states that have benefited from the 'white revolution'. It is the men who work in the fields.

The total cultivated area of the state encompasses about 20 million hectares and out of this only 20% of the land is irrigated. Ground water level is available only at a depth of 30 to 61 m. Rajasthan farmers have to depend on different sources of irrigation that include tube wells, wells and tanks. The Punjab rivers in the north, the Narmada river in the south and the Agra canals from Haryana and Uttar Pradesh provide water to the dry land of Rajasthan. Northwestern Rajasthan is irrigated by the Indira Gandhi Canal

Rajasthan has two principal crop seasons:

1. Rabi
2. Kharif

The rabi crops are winter crops and are sown in the months of October and November and are harvested in the months of March and April. The principal rabi crops are barley, wheat, gram, pulses and oil seeds. The major oil seeds are rape and mustard.

The kharif crops are the crops that are grown in the summer season and are seeded in the months of June and July. These crops are harvested in the months of September and October and include bajra, pulses, jowar, maize and ground nuts.

Three important crops grown here are wheat, corn and millets, with the last being used for baking breads in the villages, while those in larger towns show a preference for wheat flour. Pulses are another important crop, since this forms the basis of the lentils required for cooking meals. Sesame and groundnuts are grown and are important sources of cooking oil. The land is still not used for growing vegetables other than crops of potatoes, and more recently, tomatoes. Fresh vegetables have not formed a part of the traditional cuisine of the state, therefore it is still not being grown. Dehydrated vegetables—*sangri* and *gwarphali* from the bean families, and *kakri* from the cucumber family—can be eaten when fresh, or stored for use in later months, and village diets still consume these. In recent years, with transport communications between towns, the availability of fresh vegetables in towns and cities has increased.

Some places of Rajasthan that has black soil nurture the growth of major cash crops like cotton. In some regions tobacco is also grown. Apart from these crops, an assortment of fruits and vegetables are also grown in Rajasthan in the local gardens and some fertile regions. These fruits include oranges, guavas, lemons, pomegranates and mangoes.

Rajasthan soil is also suited for the growth of some spice plants, especially red, hot chillies. These chillies give Rajasthan its distinct flavour. Other spices are cumin seeds and methi.

The latter is grown under rain-fed farming conditions or in irrigated areas. Bajra is consumed by the rural poor, particularly the nomads. Rajasthan is the largest producer of bajra in India. Juar is an important pulse crop during the monsoon. Gram is another major pulse crop grown in rabi. Wheat is cultivated on irrigated land. Barley is the second largest crop in Rajasthan. Maize is a stable crop for the Bhil tribes in the Aravallis. In northern Rajasthan, maize is a delicacy eaten with butter and the green leaf of the mustard plant.

Irrigation is by electric pumps. Electricity is supplied to about 80 per cent of the villages, energising pumps and tube wells. Irrigation by the Persian Wheel method is popular in the central and eastern region where the ground water table is comparatively high. One Persian wheel can irrigate up to one hectare of land.

6.7.1 Decrease in Shifting Cultivation

Under this system of farming, the tribes would stay at a place for two years at most and come back to the same place after five years. By the time the tribe returned to the earlier place, the area would again get transformed into a thriving jungle. The Saharias grew *tilli* and *urad*. The trees would supply timber for the construction of the homes while at the same time also serving as fuel for domestic purposes. This lifestyle of the Sahariya tribe did not find favour with the Forest and Revenue Department. While the Forest Department accused the tribes of destroying the forests, the Revenue Department on the other hand, lamented the loss of revenue which it claimed was unnecessarily spent on the assessment and the measurement of freshly acquired land. At present the method of shifting cultivation no longer exists.

6.8 Recent New Problems for Tribal Land Alienation

6.8.1 Industrialisation and Mining

The Rajasthan TSP (tribal sub-plan) area under the Fifth Schedule does not allow any non-tribals to take the land of the tribals for any purposes explained earlier. In Rajasthan mining basically takes place on tribal lands. In southern Rajasthan there mining activities are carried out by non-tribals who obtain a lease from the mining department to mine in the tribal area. This is a violation of the Fifth Schedule.

A case at hand on land alienation is by the new unit established by the Binani Cement in Pindwara Block, Sirohi District. They acquired the land through the government and worse still, the community was not compensated and even the company did not recruit people from the community.

6.8.2 SEZ (Special Economic Zone)

This is another kind of land alienation today where the government acquires even fertile land to the private businesses against the wishes of the farmers. The farmers plough two to three crops in a year and it has high production capacity due to its fertility. For instance in Sitapura, the ten thousand acre fertile land that supplied all vegetable requirements to Jaipur city was give to the Mahindra and Mahindra Company. In Udaipur City, the government identified and gave permission for Stone SEZ. Due to this more than one thousand families will be displaced. The SEZ is named now to be the contributor of land alienation in the tribal areas.

6.8.3 Biofuel

The common land and green pasture areas are transferred to the private sectors. This kind of land is recorded as wasteland while off the record it is not wasteland but used by the community for various purposes. The government gives this land to the private sector without the knowledge of the Gram Sabhas who have authority at the village level. This is against public interest and results in community land alienation.

6.8.4 Highway

In the name of development the tribal lands are taken for the construction of the National Highway. As the result of this construction, the tribals are forced to leave the highway site after the survey has been conducted and recorded without the tribals' knowledge.

6.8.5 Globalisation

Globalisation and privatisation are the key focal areas of our new economic policy. This policy is being aggressively introduced in the tribal areas which are rich in natural resources in order to cater to the global corporate and private interests. As the tribal areas are safeguarded by constitutional protections like the Fifth Schedule, there is a determined attempt to violate the laws by the state itself in order to pursue its privatisation policies. Hence, there is an imminent threat to the lands and natural resources of the tribal people as well as to their customary practices and traditional rights.

Food security, potable drinking water and sanitation will be a serious crisis in the health and survival of Adivasi children as these resources will become less accessible to tribal communities due to their commercialisation. According to the three years survey made by ASTHA in tribal areas in Rajasthan, it was found that the percentage of families who took loans 'in the previous year' declined from 56% in Year I to 42% in Year II, and increased to 49% in Year III. It was further observed that increasing income of the families leads to increasing indebtedness. The incidence of taking loans decreased in all sample families where poverty increased or stagnated. Less poverty, more loans—more poverty, less loans.

Table 8: Some Data on Per Family Credit Taken by Families Who Took Credit

District	*Year I*	*Year II*	*Year III*
Jaipur	Rs. 12,194	Rs. 13,280	Rs. 18,817
Chittor	Rs. 10,639	Rs. 14,570	Rs. 17,908
Jhalawar	Rs. 7,992	Rs. 8,555	Rs. 6,300
Barmer	Rs. 6,486	Rs. 9,970	Rs. 7,882
Udaipur	Rs. 2,647	Rs. 4,237	Rs. 4,570

All these figures are high, for poor people. Indebtedness is a way of life, it seems. A look at the different reasons for taking loans, the percentage of amounts taken for different purposes, and the total rupee amount taken by families in the study sample is presented below:

Table 9: The Reasons for Taking Loans, and the Percentage of Total Loans Taken for Each Stated Purpose

Purposes	*Year I*	*Year II*
Purchase of Income Generating Items	23.64%	26.00%
Social Obligations	25.00%	25.21%
Home Expenses	16.65%	23.66%
Illness	8.86%	10.21%
Repay Outstanding Debts	5.81%	3.88 %
Purchase of Consumer Durables	2.61%	2.72 %
Education	1.20%	0.17%
Other	6.85%	8.18%

7

Violation of Recognition of Forest Rights Act

A sizeable number of the tribal community lives in the forest areas of Rajasthan and their livelihood is dependent on forests. A major portion of their total income comes from forests, their livelihood activities include collecting forest produce, agricultural work on forest land in their possession and animal husbandry.

Based on the latest government statistics, more than one lakh tribal families are directly dependent on forest land and indirectly all rural tribals are dependent on forests which is 12% of the state's total population.

After the enforcement of Recognition of Forest Rights Act in the country it was anticipated that in Rajasthan too tribals will be protected from displacement from forest areas and dispossession from their traditional forest rights will be protected. However, after enforcement of this Act, the tribal community has not received any relief.

Since the enforcement of the Act from January 1, 2008, the Government of Rajasthan has abused the basic spirit of this law and started defining and implementing it as per their own convenience misleading the Forest Department, Panchayati Raj Department, Revenue Department and Scheduled Tribes Department.

Negative Approach of Forest Department

Possessing forests for approximately 140 years, the Forest

Department is not prepared to relinquish their control over forests. The Forest Department continues to resist the implementation of this law using all their might.

In order to prevent the implementation of this Act, the Forest Department has adopted many devious ways to create problems to the people; various examples have come up after January 1, 2008.

- Preparation of unauthorised claim documents parallel to valid claim documents.
- Getting signatures on blank papers from people for voluntarily relinquishing their possession.
- Extortion in the name of verification.
- Recording less possession than actual possession of land at the time of verification.
- Asking people to write that they do not have any right on forests on community rights claim forms.
- Evicting claimants before disposing of their claims.
- Not implementing forest rights in forest enclosures, sanctuaries, and national parks.
- Insisting on penalty receipt for forest offences as evidence for accepting claims on forest land by the Forest Department.
- Forest Department constructing walls around the forest while forest dwellers claims are pending over the same area.
- Getting the recommendation from the forest rights committees without following the procedures required under rule 12 of the Act which requires proper inquiry and physical verification of each claim.
- Accepting only those claims which are mentioned in the encroachers list of the Forest Department.

Irregularities at Panchayat Level

- Arbitrarily bringing in their own people as members of Forest Rights Committee.
- Causing disappearance of claim files.
- Not organising Gram Sabhas despite requests from

claimants and Gram Sabha members. Gram Sabha meetings are important for forwarding forest land claims to the Sub-Divisional Committee.

- In place of the village, organising Gram Sabha meetings at Panchayat level.

Patwaries *(Government accountants for land records) Troubling Claimants*

- Informing wrong plot *(khasra)* numbers
- Recording land areas based on information provided by the Forest Department
- Not providing revenue records of claimants
- Confusing claimants by informing revenue land as forest land
- Not being present when field verifications are conducted by the Forest Rights Committees despite requests from the Committees.
- Forest Department falsifying facts by claiming that the claimant is not in possession of the forest land or the occupation is a fresh encroachment.

Apathy of Sub-Divisional Committee

- Not providing claim forms to claimants
- Not providing documents despite demand for the same by the Forest Rights Committee and Gram Sabhas
- Not resolving boundary disputes between two villages or panchayats
- Illegal rejection of claims based on recommendations of the Forest Department
- Not encouraging villagers to document their traditional knowledge and maintain the bio-diversity register
- Not ensuring the cooperation of the Secretary of the Gram Panchayat
- Not providing information to claimants regarding rejected claims

- Rejecting claims without verifying them
- Not publicizing and promoting the law
- Not providing training to Forest Rights Committees

At District Level Committees

- Issuing title for land for a lesser area than in actual possession and claimed
- Disposing claims based upon Forest Department's recommendations
- Considering claims of only those with fine receipts of forest offence of encroachment issued by the Forest Department.
- Not organising timely district level meetings.

State Level Monitoring Committee

- Not organising regular meetings as per rules.
- Not resolving complaints of claimants.
- Not monitoring whether the implementation is as per the law and its rules in its true spirit.
- Not ensuring that the committees have the requisite membership from the elected Panchayat representatives.

Illegal Activities at Government Level

- Not accepting claims of non-tribal forest dwellers and from municipal areas.
- Not providing claim forms to claimants.
- Instructing formation of Forest Rights Committees in Scheduled Areas at revenue village level and in non-Scheduled Areas at Panchayat level.
- Notifying new national parks and wildlife sanctuaries before completing forest rights recognition and recognizing forest rights claims. Example: Notification of Kumbhalgarh National Park and on-going plans to evict people from Kotra and Jhadol Talukas (Tehsil) of Udaipur district.

Forest Rights Act could be an effective instrument for

asserting their forest land rights by poor tribals; but for reasons mentioned above they are deprived of their individual and collective rights on forest land. As per data of the Tribal Development Department, Udaipur, till 30 September 2013 69,686 claims were submitted to Gram Sabhas of which 30,770 claims (42%) were rejected and in 33,696 cases titles were issued.

But the titles issued did not exceed two *Bigha* land which is insufficient for the livelihood of people and violates the forest rights act. There has also not been any progress on recognising community forest rights. Only 60 titles have been issued for claims under Section 3 (2) for one hectare land for development work of providing basic amenities like; hospital, anganwadi, anicut, canal, electricity line, community centre, school for the village. Hundreds of community rights claims were prepared by the people but these are not disposed off. On the other hand the Forest Department is constructing permanent walls on community land and taking it into their possession denying individual and community rights over the lands by preventing access to the lands.

People Unfriendly Jatropha Policy

In the context of forest rights, the Jatropha policy is becoming an important issue for tribals. Already the tribals have lost most of their forests and the Jatropha Policy is going to add to their sufferings. On 10 January 2007, the Government of Rajasthan issued a cabinet notification. As per this letter, the state's barren land can be used for cultivation of oil plants and for this purpose lease can be granted to private companies up to five thousand hectares land.

While the government on the one hand is implementing laws such as the Forest Rights Act, on the other hand the government is planning to allocate for 50 lakhs hectare of the one crore barren land in the State for producing bio-fuel. 14.5 lakhs hectare land is to be allotted to private companies on lease. But these are lands which are occupied by poor farmers whose livelihood is based on these lands. Instead of recognizing tenurial rights of those dependent on these lands, the government is planning to give these lands to private companies free of cost.

Twenty-one companies have submitted their applications for allotment of 30 lakh hectare lands. It is clear that good quality and best lands will be provided to these private companies. Considering the increased possibility of production of Jatropha and similar oil plants on barren lands which is capable of producing bio fuel, Biofuel Mission under the chairpersonship of the Chief Minister was set up in 2005-06. The objectives of this mission includes cultivation of Jatropha, Karanj and other similar oil plants, conduct research, proper processing, marketing and ensuring basic facilities in this regard. According to the government, this mission will be helpful in development of these barren lands, employment generation, new direction for industrial development and thereby reducing poverty in rural areas. But actually this is a conspiracy for evicting the poor from the lands under their possession. Barren land will be allotted to registered public and private companies registered under the Indian Companies Act 1956, societies registered under the Rajasthan Societies Registration Act 1958, and those capable of its development and production. Other than this category, barren land will be allotted to BPL savings and credit groups, Panchayati Raj institutions and cooperative societies. Land useful for cultivation of Jatropha and other similar oil plants can be allotted to categories that include families living below the poverty line, Self Help Groups (SHG) formed under the Swarn Jayanti Gram Swarojgar Yojana (SGSY) and Women's Self Help Groups. There is a precondition, that these groups should be registered as members as landless farmers under the Land Revenue (Land Allotment for Agricultural Scheme) Rule 1970.

Land allotment to public sector enterprises, private companies and registered societies will be done on the basis of 20 years lease and allotment for remaining categories will be done on the basis of non-tenancy of land. On allotted land allotees would do 50% plantation during the first two years and the remaining allotted land will be used for plantation from the third year onwards. It seems that the state government has framed the biofuel policy sitting in a room considering them to be positive though impractical. However, there are numerous questions that are untouched that lead to skepticism which cannot be ignored.

These are enumerated as under:

1. From where is government going to get the proposed amount of barren land to be allotted? There are bushes on 30% land of 1 crore hectares of barren land; existence of these bushes are not surprising in a dry state like Rajasthan. These bushes are the lifeline for a large number of the state's rural population as their livestock especially sheep, goats and camels are dependent on this.
2. The quality of 28% of land is such that plantation of biofuel plants are going to be very expensive and less beneficial.
3. On the remaining land, there are meadows or forest land.
4. There are barren lands which may be available on revenue records but actually they are under the possession of many families; there are large numbers of land of this nature. Whether the District Collector is going to give priority to this and take note that these lands are under the possession of landless people and that they have invested their hard labour and money on these lands is doubtful.
5. Regarding framing and enforcement of this policy, inputs have been sought from concerned government departments such as finance, forests, rural development, etc. However, this plan has not been communicated to those whose lands are proposed to be taken up, the Gram Sabhas, and Panchayats. No inputs or suggestions have been sought from them.

It seems that the state government is in a hurry to allot these lands to companies only, which is not at all in public interest.

6. The Forest Department has raised concerns regarding use of forests for non-forestry purposes. In this regard they have also written to the state government. The state government's response to these concerns is not known. Also from the environmental point of view this does not seem sensible.
7. The Finance Department has also sent an objection letter to the rural development department; they have sought information about the list of allottees and progress in this regard. The Finance Department has also objected to not maintaining records to the nodal agency - Rajasthan State Industrial Development and Investment Corporation.
8. Maximum limit of land allotment is unclear. At present there is a provision for allotment of 500 hectares. In special cases it could be 1000 hectares which is for bio-fuel production. However, for agricultural produce there is a ceiling of 500 hectares. This difference is unclear. Therefore it is difficult to understand the actual objectives of this policy.
9. Land has been allotted to various units; whether they will establish processing plants or not, it is not clear.
10. Other than this there is lack of clarity regarding institutions registered under Societies Act, cooperative societies and Panchayati Raj institutions and if they would be benefited under the Land Allotment Scheme or not. The Finance Department has clearly written that government has too little control on these institutions. Therefore, land should not be allotted to them.
11. What would be the density regarding plantation is unclear. In this regard it is not known to what extent the Forest Department is involved.
12. Regarding plantation of Jatropha areas with suitable

climate have been identified. This is the south eastern part of Rajasthan where temperature is below 45 degrees and rainfall is above 500 milliliters. From this it is clear that for plantation of Jatropha sufficient water and a suitable climate is necessary; only then can desired production be achieved. However, this region has high bio-diversity and forests, where this kind of plantation will adversely affect the climate. In such a favourable environment a farmer can very well produce other traditional crops.

13. From 3.5 kilogram Jatropha seeds 1 kilogram biodiesel can be extracted and that diesel could not be sold for more than Rs. 25/- per kilogram. Therefore, it is clear that seeds should be purchased at the rate of Rs. 4 to 5 per kilogram. This will become the reason for exploitation of farmers because the present rate of seeds is Rs. 8 to 10 per kilogram.
14. Besides this, farmers will be forced to sell their seeds to companies or RAJFED or RAJAS Sangh[1] which is direct violation of Recognition of Forest Rights Act and PESA Act.
15. In this situation farmers or companies will increase the area of Jatropha plantation so that they can produce more and overcome their losses. Then other traditional plants would have to cut down which will not be suitable from bio-diversity's perspective and it will promote monoculture (single forestation).
16. The production cost of one hectare Jatropha plantation comes up to Rs. 25,000/- and Rs. 5,000/- per year is required for its maintenance. During the first two years, there is no income from it and income of the third and fourth year is also insufficient. In the fifth year this becomes rewarding. It also depends upon favourable conditions, cost of irrigation,

1.Rajasthan Tribal Area Development Cooperative Federation Ltd.

fertilisers, maintenance and weather is also significant. However, in the first year Rs. 7,500/- per hectare is given as grant, in the second year it is Rs.1,500/-, for farmers, Panchayati Raj Institutions and cooperative societies there is a provision for allotment of 10 hectare land. Whether is it possible for a farmer living below the poverty line to invest Rs. 1,50,000, in case he is unable to meet these costs, then what would be the loan policy, and whether they would not come under a huge debt.

17. Without adequate research, will it be sensible and beneficial for long-term development of Jatropha to implement this policy? For development of oil rich, high production, less water consuming and faster maturity species of plants, till now no activity has taken place nor is it determined whether this is possible at all.
18. For large-scale plantation and production of Jatropha there is a scheme for promotion of big industrialists to use contractual-based cropping. With this, it is clear that the government will prefer private companies and because of contractual schemes there is enough scope for farmers' economic exploitation.
19. There is a plan to keep loan facilities transparent and people-friendly. This leads to the question whether loan policies were transparent and people-friendly in the past, if not, then there is a big doubt about it.
20. According to the Forest Conservation Act 1980, planting of oil producing plants are non-forest activities.
21. In 1990, prohibition was imposed on Rajasthan Land Revenue (allotment of barren lands for private forest development) Rule 1986. This prohibition should be removed because the rule was hardly implemented. Also any significant effort for allotment of land to eligible poor farmers, Gram Panchayats, Cooperative Societies is not known. However, under this scheme

afforestation could have been done on allotted lands and desired benefits could have been given to people. The state government was also able to generate desired revenue from this and a large section of rural population may have benefited because of low production cost, as there is provision for one hectare allotment per BPL family and not more than five hectares in other cases.

22. General interpretation of 'barren land' is that it is land which has never been cultivated. It is difficult to establish this. Cultivation has been done on these barren lands but has not been recorded in land revenue records.
23. Composition of committees for identification of barren land is as follows:
    - District Collector: President
    - General Manager of District Industrial Centre: Member
    - District Agriculture Officer: Member
    - MLA: Member

    There is no representation from the Gram Sabha and local people in this committee. In the name of people's representation there is the MLA, who is generally not associated with people directly and there is no clarity for ensuring people's participation in it.
24. List of identified villages in districts to whom land will be allotted has not been made public, this needs to be done and the concerned villages should be informed.
25. There is a provision for subsidy of Rs.10,000/- per hectare and lease rent per hectare is Rs.400/-. This difference seems strange, it appears that each allottee is provided Rs. 9,600/- as a free gift.
26. In the southern part of the state, especially in tribal areas, there are degraded forest lands and thousands are in possession of these lands and this possession is with them prior to 13 December 2005. The

framework has not been laid down regarding regulation of these lands. Therefore, this scheme should not be implemented in these areas as this will lead to a number of disputes. Under the Forest Rights Act claims to these lands are still pending.

27. Allottees will have to complete 50% plantation on allotted land during the first two years and on the remaining lands planting will have to be completed by the third year; otherwise their allotments will be considered cancelled. In this regard required preparations of concerned departments are not visible. For example, the Forest Department has not readied their nursery, and the Finance Department has not made arrangements for funds. There is no transparent and people-friendly loan policy in place. Regarding subsidy, other than broad information, there is no clarity, neither have any type of trainings been provided nor is any literature available on this. In these circumstances companies will be in a position to achieve their targets but Panchayats, BPL groups, etc. will not be able to achieve their targets and they would lose their allotments and get trapped under debt.
28. In Udaipur district a total of 4,11,337 hectare land have been earmarked under this scheme, which is 37% of total 14,62,105 hectare land available in the district. If we assume that 50% of these lands are degraded forest which is approximately 2,05,668.5 hectares and on half of these lands there are very old occupation of people. Actually there is insufficient land to be allotted under this policy. This is the story in other districts as well.

Lease Rent

For allotted land annual lease rent will be based on the following grounds:

- There will not be any lease rent for the first year of

allotment

- From the second year to fifth year of allotment, there will be a lease rent of Rs. 125/- per hectare
- After fifth year to tenth year of allotment, there will be a lease rent of Rs. 200/- per hectare
- After the tenth year to fifteenth year of allotment, there will be a lease rent of Rs. 400/- per hectare
- After the fifteenth year of allotment, the government will do a revaluation for lease allotments.

The size of the allotted land could be 500 to 1000 hectares. The concerned Committee, which is headed by the District Collector can allot land up to 100 hectares to other groups. These conditions are bizarre because for developing these lands the central government is providing a subsidy and private companies will be benefited from this. Hence, companies are getting land free and additional subsidy from government for its development. Companies will have to establish oil extraction plants. In this regard all the Collectors have been directed to identify lands. With this analysis, one can assume that government is hurriedly taking decisions on people-unfriendly schemes. For so many years people have been in possession of these lands and they will not be prepared to relinquish their rights. Against such people-unfriendly decisions, an indefinite demonstration was held in the Udaipur division. This demonstration began from July 16, 2006 and ended on 30 July 2006. Prior to this, the government invited applications from various companies and for getting these lands, a number of organisations and Self Help Groups emerged overnight. Government started allotting people's lands for plantation of Jatropha. But people without formal recognition of their entitlements have been cultivating these lands for years. These are either forest land or donated land, allotted land to landless farmers or allotted land under any scheme. These are now allotted by government for plantation of Jatropha. In this backdrop, the above mentioned demonstration was held in Udaipur and it was effective and forced government to shift this scheme and put it on the backburner.

Tribal Self-Governance Act

In order to preserve tribal culture and management of resources through traditional methods, in 1996 the central government introduced the Tribal self-governance act, namely the Panchayat (Extension to Scheduled Areas) Act, 1996. Though the State government made amendments to the existing State Panchayat Raj Act within a year, rules were not notified for over a decade. Tribal organizations put pressure on the government and filed a petition in the High Court. Subsequently, the government framed rules but these rules do not express the true spirit of the Act, as it has given all the powers to government officers and Sarpanchs. Now Gram Sabhas have become a machinery which is under the control of the government officials only.

Government of Rajasthan enforced these rules on 1 November 2011. It is mentioned that these rules have been framed for effective implantation of Panchayat (Extension to Scheduled Areas) Act (PESA) and these rules have been laid down based upon basic spirit of the Act. On the other hand, in each chapter the true spirit of the Act has been compromised. The term Gram Sabha has not been defined and there is lack of clarity about its meaning.

- What would be the boundary/limitation of a Gram Sabha has not been mentioned, area/jurisdiction of Gram Sabha has been pointed out only.
- What is a village has also not been clarified.
- All rights have been given to the Forest Department regarding forest produce but it is silent on its ownership rights. It seems that the Gram Sabha is only expected to follow instructions of government officers.
- No rights have been provided regarding protection, conservation and management of forests, instead the Forest Department has been strengthened.
- Provisions have been made in a way that without

permission of the Forest Department not a single leaf can be removed. Even to this extent that forest produce will be sold to RJS Union based on the supported rate of the RJS Union under the supervision of the Forest Department. All rights of bamboos and tendu leaves have been kept with the Forest Department and the remaining minor forest produce have to be collected through 'the village protection and management committee or RAJAS Sangh or Cooperative Societies'

- Regarding mining, all rights have been given to mining engineers, not a single type of right has been given to the Gram Sabha.
- Regarding organising of a Gram Sabha and its proceedings, decision-making rights have been given to Panchayats.
- All powers of Gram Sabha have been taken away and it has become a mere recommendatory body.
- It seems that, according to the PESA Act changes have not been made in the functioning of other departments. Actually PESA rules have been framed based on convenience of concerned government departments, which is a direct violation of the PESA.
- For preservation of good practices of a village and based on that functioning and managing affairs of a village system has not been mentioned anywhere.

8

Conclusion

The protective legislation shows several defects in implementation. The Urban Land Conversion Rules, 1981, have been quite widely subverted as once the ST gets the land converted, the same land is sold by registration. The leases based on sharecropping are never recorded in the land records. Adverse possession through Benami sale transactions and the leasing out prevail. Land alienation exists more through the absence of physical possession than due to absence of legal title. Sharecropping with the moneylenders to repay old mortgages reduces the *Khatedar* tribals to the status of sub-tenants. The effectiveness of the administration in studying and identifying concealed tenancy through adverse possession against tribals has decreased to a great extent. Problems have arisen owing to the collusion of the Patwari with the powerful sections of the village. Acquisition of tribal land, and diversion of forest and community land further compounds land alienation.

Collusion of officials such as the Patwari and lack of legal knowledge at the lower ranks of administration are also major problems faced. Maximum land alienation exists due to adverse and concealed physical possessions.

In the absence of advancing consumption loans to the tribals through institutional agencies, it is difficult to abolish the institution of moneylending. Increased consumption loans, and lack of support to check usury increases land alienation.

Effective operationalisation of PESA provisions in the state and strong and sustained involvement of people's organisations in the identification of alienation of tribal land and its restoration appears to be important remedial measures.

One of the major problems faced by the tribals is the effect of displacement due to construction of major and minor irrigation dams. In some of the cases the compensation to the tribals who are displaced is given in the form of land in distant villages, which uproots them both economically and socially. Many who are displaced are still in a dilemma. No project should be undertaken till the process of land allocation and rehabilitation of the tribals are completed.

One of the major concerns emerging in this context of urbanisation is that the tribal lands next to urban complexes are being transferred to non-tribals for a song resulting in deprivations to the tribals. The industrialisation and mining activities adversely impact tribals with land alienation. A comprehensive survey should be undertaken to identify the extent of tribal lands affected so that remedial actions may be identified and initiated.

Despite the ban in agricultural tenancies in most states, the incidence of this type of tenancy, particularly in various forms of crop sharing is still substantial in some regions. As tenancy is contracted orally in most cases in violation of the law, such a tiller's position remains precarious. He has no incentive to cultivate land efficiently. In several regions, the landowners keep their land fallow for fear of losing their rights if they let it out illegally. It also restricts poor people's access to land through leasing in. Currently, there is no appropriate legal system for recording such cases of tilling arrangements. Also there is a growing problem of reverse tenancy.

Bibliography

1. Agarwal, Bina, 1994a. *A Field of One's Own: Gender and Land Rights in South Asia*, Cambridge: Cambridge University Press.
2. Bhasin, M.K. and Shampa Nag, 2007. Demography of the Tribal Groups of Rajasthan: 1, Population Structure. *Anthropologist*, 9(1): 1-37.
3. Centre for Policy Dialogue. Gender, Land and Livelihood in South Asia, Report No. 30, Website: www.cpd-bangladesh.org
4. Chand, Tara, 1972. *History of the Freedom Movement in India*, 4 vols., New Delhi.
5. Ekal Nari Shakti Sangathan, 2004. 'AARAMBH'—A Beginning ....A Beginning of a Widows' Land Rights Movement, Udaipur, Rajasthan.
6. Hardiman, David , August 1996. Usury, Death, and Famine in Western India, *Past & Present*.
7. Hegde, N.C. Community Pasture Development Programme in Rajasthan. A Sustainable Model for Livelihood.
8. Jain, P.C., 1989. *Tribal Agrarian Movement*, Himanshu Publications, Udaipur.
9. Land Research Action Network, January 21, 2003. Backgrounder Part II— *Land Reform in India, Issues and Challenges*.
10. Pande, R., 1980. Appraisal of Land Reforms.
11. Pankaj Ballabh. National Foundation for India (ed.), 2004. *Land, Community and Governance*, New Delhi.
12. Sharma, B.K., 1996. *Tribal Revolts*. Pointer Publishers, Jaipur.
13. State of Environment Report for Rajasthan, 2007. Chapter 7, Tourism Sector.

14. The Resettlement of Project Affected People, "Is 'Bigger' Better, or is 'Small' Beautiful?" Displacement and Resettlement, RIPA, Jaipur.
15. Yugandhar, B.N. and P.S. Datta (eds), 1995. *Land Reforms in India*, Vol. 2: *Rajasthan; Feudalism and Change*. New Delhi: Sage Publications India Pvt. Ltd.